A FATHER'S STORY

Published by Echo Point Books & Media
Brattleboro, Vermont
www.EchoPointBooks.com

A Father's Story
ISBN: 978-1-64837-053-3 (casebound)
          978-1-63561-563-0 (paperback)

Second Edition

Interior design by MM Design 2000, Inc. / Michael Mendelsohn

Cover design by Adrienne Núñez

A FATHER'S STORY

LIONEL DAHMER

ECHO POINT BOOKS & MEDIA, LLC
Brattleboro, Vermont

It is my desire that something positive will result from all the sorrow inflicted upon so many people by Jeff's actions. It is in the spirit of this desire, and in sincerest sympathy, that I intend to donate a portion of the proceeds from this book to benefit victims' families. While no donation can atone for such tremendous loss, I hope that what little I am able to do will help in some way.

FOREWORD
to the Echo Point Books Edition

After its initial publication, great reviews, and burst of national publicity, *A Father's Story,* reached a large audience, selling hundreds of thousands of copies. Inevitably, though, the media spotlight moved on to other news stories, the attention died down, and the pace of book sales slowed. Eventually, the large publishers who published and distributed this work, decided to let the book go out of print. Reader interest, however, never disappeared. In a classic example of what happens when demand exceeds supply, prices paid online for *A Father's Story* surged to hundreds of dollars for a single copy. Even used copies in poor condition rarely fell below $50. Based on this sustained interest, it seemed clear the book needed to be republished. In February of 2017, we signed a contract with Mr. Dahmer to reissue his memoir.

Before publishing *A Father's Story,* Lionel indicated he wanted to make some small changes to the book to correct some subtle—and not so subtle—distortions that appeared in the previous edition. We readily agreed to work with him to publish the most accurate book possible.

Soon after signing our contract it became clear that it was going to take a while to make these changes; in fact, quite a while. Although we regularly checked in with Lionel about the edits he wished to make, month after month, year after year, there was little to show for our phone calls and email reminders. A big reason for the lack of progress was that Lionel was battling poor health (at this writing he is 84) and his wife—whom he takes care of—is very ill. Even her aide got cancer. This made it difficult for him to focus on his memoir. But from my perspective, that was only part of the reason.

As I worked with Lionel and developed his trust, it became clear to me that even though he and his household faced daunting health challenges, there were also strong emotional blocks to revisiting this work. Of course, nothing compares to the pain and anguish of Jeffery Dahmer's victims and their families, but even if someone else is suffering from more agony than you, great pain is still great pain. Who could blame Lionel for hesitating before doing a deep dive into reviewing and articulating his thoughts about Jeffrey yet again? Who in his or her wildest nightmare, would want to find themselves in his position? The pain and anguish over Jeffrey's actions would crush most spirits. Few of us could imagine what it would be like to have someone you love, your own flesh and blood, your baby and little boy, who you raised with all the hopes and dreams all parents have, turn into one of the most notorious and gruesome serial killers of all time.

It took almost four years, but eventually we made the changes Lionel wanted. In the context of the whole book, these edits were small, but they give greater clarity about who Lionel is and thus a little better understanding of Jeffrey Dahmer and his actions. Although Lionel's memoir is just one aspect of a multi-layered and extreme tragedy, he does have a unique perspective for anyone interested in Jeffrey Dahmer's crimes, his upbringing, and how families deal with criminal behavior. What it is like to be the father of a son whose name is synonymous with depraved killing? What can his and Jeffrey's life tell us about the ongoing debates over nature versus nurture? These are hard questions to wrestle with and it is brave of Lionel to share his life and experiences so openly. I can attest that it has been difficult for him to talk and write about his experiences, but his efforts have been worthwhile. I am confident you will find this book engaging and valuable reading.

Marshall Glickman
PUBLISHER, ECHO POINT BOOKS & MEDIA
FEBRUARY, 2021

ACKNOWLEDGMENTS

The names of friends, acquaintances, and strangers who supported Shari and me throughout this darkest period of our lives are much more numerous than the people who showed ill will toward us. We desperately needed the understanding words and prayers.

Although I have never met Patrick Kennedy, I have been told that he treated Jeff as a human being during the long questioning periods immediately following the arrest. I express my gratitude to him and to his partner in the Milwaukee Detective Bureau, Dennis Murphy, whom I did meet and respect for his like behavior toward Jeff and me.

Shari has a very special spot in her memory of Captain M. Gurich, Patrol Division of the Medina, Ohio, County Sheriff's Department and his two deputies, who came to inform her of Jeff's arrest. She remembers Captain Gurich gently breaking the details to her as he sat on the couch in our home. Also, my thanks to all of the sheriff's staff for their assistance on a moment's notice to protect my wife from harassment from the press and media.

During Jeff's court appearance in Akron, Ohio, in May 1992, Sheriff Troutman, John Karabatsos, and all the associate deputies exhibited extremely gracious and humane treatment toward Jeff, Shari, and me.

Being a longtime resident of Bath, Ohio, and participating with many of the members of the Bath Fire and Rescue Squad in Indian guides, T-Ball, etc., I learned early of the efficiency and dedication of the Bath Police Department, and of the caring nature of Chief Gravis. The degree of professionalism and sensitivity exhibited by Detective Lt. Richard Munsey of the Bath Police, as he handled various aspects of the investigation, was exceptional, and will not be forgotten.

A special thanks is also due to Kenneth Risse of the West Allis, Wisconsin, Police Department for prompt and extraordinary response to my frequent calls for patrol cars to control the assault on my mother's home and property by the media. His young patrolman, Jacques Chevreman, guarded my mother's property as if it were his own mother's place. To the kind and helpful neighbors, who brought food and comfort, I give thanks for my mother.

Both Shari and I have been heartened and enriched as a result of continuing dialogue with Theresa Smith, a caring sister of Eddie Smith. We have appreciated her concern and sensitivity.

I would be remiss not to acknowledge and thank

Ed Gernon, a screenwriter in Los Angeles, for starting me on the book project. Also, to Nancy Snyder, for her continued and constant support in our troubled times, I say a very warm and heartfelt thank you.

With great affection, gratitude, and respect, I acknowledge attorneys Robert and Joyce Mozenter of Philadelphia, Larry Vuillemin of Akron, and Steve Eisenberg of Madison, with Larry Vuillemin as Jeff's and our attorney for legal affairs connected with the Akron and Ohio area, and with Steve Eisenberg handling all legal affairs in Wisconsin. We wish to acknowledge them for their tremendous contributions in assisting both Jeff and us in all legal matters after the Milwaukee trial. Since these people have come on board, we now feel that we have a strong, caring, cohesive team.

I will be forever grateful to Dick and Tom Jungck of New Berlin, Wisconsin. These twin brother lifelong friends were the first to reach out to me in all my confusion as I arrived in Milwaukee, July 24, 1991. They, including Sandy and Karen, and their homes, were havens where Shari and I could gather our thoughts and make plans throughout this long ordeal. Whether giving advice or extensive physical help, they were always there for me, Shari, and my mother.

To Thomas H. Cook, I owe my deep gratitude for his personal commitment to see this most difficult project to its completion.

For my agent Joel Gotler and his Renaissance Agency staff in Los Angeles, California, I am very much indebted for insightful advice and efficient, rapid response, especially during the frustrating, uncertain times before completion of this book. Joel has shown his concern for us as individuals, while demonstrating his professionalism as a business person with excellent contacts.

From the first meeting with the William Morrow Publishing Company in New York City, I felt that Senior Editor Paul Bresnick and his staff were interested in a story that would be from an entirely different vantage point. I thank Paul for his commitment to this book and for his considerate flexibility during some initial problems. I am very grateful that William Morrow and Paul allowed me the opportunity to explore the relationships intertwining my background with Jeff's, to shed some light on how he developed, and to show that he was not, as some people insist, born a monster.

To Dr. Robert Kirkhart, a clinical psychologist, in Cuyahoga Falls, Ohio, I express my deepest gratitude for helping Shari and me through our pain and grief during the ordeal of these last two years. He is truly a model of wisdom, caring, and patience.

To a very dear relative who chooses to be anonymous, I will always remember the understanding and great help you gave me, you who loves as my mother loved.

Finally, I reserve until last two very important persons in my life. One, who is very much alive but whose health has been permanently altered by this ordeal, my wife, Shari. This book could not have been written without the immense assistance of Shari. It was her memory, her insight, and her sensitivity that made it possible. She is the epitome of a tremendously caring helpmate who will give her all to protect her own. The other person is my mother, who just a few months ago succumbed to the ravages of this ordeal. Catherine Dahmer, an unwitting victim, loved Jeff and me without reservation, unconditionally. The degree of love and the quality of family experiences that she and my devoted father, Herbert Dahmer, shared with me could be a standard, I think, for parents everywhere. The reason that I write of Shari and Catherine together is that they had formed a bond that was special, especially strong in these later years. Tears immediately stream from Shari's eyes when mention is made of the special things Catherine would do for Jeff, the love she felt for him, the fact that she would literally give her life for Jeff or me. These are two very dear women.

—LIONEL H. DAHMER
Akron, Ohio

In deep and awful channel runs
This sympathy for Sire and Sons
—William Wordsworth

PART I

If the police had told me that my son was dead, I would have thought differently about him. If they'd told me that a strange man had lured him to a seedy apartment, and a few minutes later, drugged, strangled, then sexually assaulted and mutilated his dead body—in other words, if they'd told *me* the same horrible things that they had to tell so many other fathers and mothers in July of 1991, then I would have done what they have done. I would have mourned my son and demanded that the man who'd killed him be profoundly punished. If not executed, then separated forever from the rest of us. After that, I would have tried to think of my son warmly. I would, I hope, have visited his grave from time to time, spoken of him with loss and affection, continued, as much as possible, to be the custodian of his memory.

But I wasn't told what these other mothers and fathers were told, that their sons were dead at the hands of a murderer. Instead, I was told that *my* son was the one who had murdered *their* sons.

And so, my son was still alive. I couldn't bury him.

I couldn't remember him fondly. He was not a figure of the past. He was still with me, as he still is.

Initially, of course, I couldn't believe that it was really Jeff who had done the things the police had accused him of. How could anyone believe that his son could do such things? I had been in the actual places where they said he had done them. I had been in rooms and basements which at other moments, according to the police, had been nothing less than a slaughterhouse. I had looked in my son's refrigerator and seen only a scattering of milk cartons and soda cans. I had leaned casually on the black table they claimed my son had used both as a dissecting table and a bizarre Satanic altar. How was it possible that all of this had been hidden from me—not only the horrible physical evidence of my son's crimes, but the dark nature of the man who had committed them, this child I had held in my arms a thousand times, and whose face, when I glimpsed it in the newspapers, looked like mine?

Predictably, as the evidence accumulated and became increasingly ghastly, I made myself believe that Jeff could not have done such things on his own, but that he had acted only as the tool of someone else, someone more evil than my son, someone who had taken advantage of Jeff's loneliness and isolation, and had turned him into a terrible slave. I conjured visions of this "other" that were probably as Satanic as the ones in Jeff's imagination. The "other" was an evil genius and manipulator, a diabolical Svengali who had lured my son into the circle of his power, and then converted him into a mindless demon. As I allowed myself to imagine such a person, the air around me seemed to fill with darting, screeching bats, and I accepted, although briefly, a world that was as hideous and malevolent as the things my son had done.

But I am an analytical thinker, and so, no matter how much I might have wanted to believe in the reality of this demonic "other," I had to accept that it was no more than a phantom I had created to protect my son, to remove some part of the blame that had been heaped upon him.

And so, my first confrontation was with myself, with the fact that I am an analytical person. I deal in real things, not things that are imagined. Evidence is evidence, and it has to be recognized as such. There was no evidence that anyone had ever made Jeff kill anyone. There was no evidence that anyone had ever helped him do such things. There wasn't even any evidence that anyone had known what Jeff was doing. His neighbors had smelled disgusting odors coming from his apartment, but none of them had ever gone inside. They had watched as Jeff came and went from his apartment, always closing the door quickly, so that no one could get a glimpse inside, but none of them had ever had the slightest suspicion of the horrors that lay behind that closed door.

Jeff had done everything alone, everything in secret. No one was to blame for all these deaths but him, and there was no question but that I had to accept that fact. Jeff had done it all. He alone was to blame.

So that was what the police really told me in July of 1991. Not that my son was dead, but that something inside of him was dead, that part which should have made him think about the misery he was causing, and so draw back from causing it.

This part is alive in most people, at least to some degree. True, everyone is selfish at times. Everyone is vain and egocentric to some extent. But in most people, there is a line that this part commands us not to cross. It tells us that we can go only so far in the way we treat other people, only so far in the way we damage them. It may be that this "part" is no more than a chemical trace or a configuration of brain cells. We call it "conscience," "being human," or "having a heart." Religious people may think it comes from God. Sociologists may think it comes from moral training. I don't know. I can only repeat what the evidence clearly suggested, that in my son it had either died or had never been alive in the first place.

In the beginning, that was my most profound admission, that there was something missing in Jeff, the part that should have cried out, *Stop!*

Jeff, catching his breath and giggling, as Lionel lifts him up and down, 1960

Jeff held lovingly by his mother, Van Buren apartment, 1960

CHAPTER ONE

My son Jeff was born in Milwaukee on May 21, 1960. It had not been an easy pregnancy. My wife had gotten pregnant very quickly, only two months after our marriage, and neither of us, I suppose, was really prepared for it. During the first part of her pregnancy, Joyce began to suffer from morning sickness, and as time went on, it steadily worsened into a more or less continual state of nausea, one so severe that she found it difficult to keep any food down at all. Her continual vomiting even affected her ability to work, and she finally found it necessary to quit her job as a teletype instructor.

After that, Joyce remained at home, coping as best she could, not only with nausea, but with other ailments, as well, both physical and emotional.

As the weeks passed, Joyce became increasingly nervous. Everything seemed to bother her, but particularly the noise and cooking odors that came from the family below us in the small two-family apartment building in which we lived. She found the slightest noise unbearable, and every odor, regardless of how ordinary, was insufferable to her. She continually demanded that I do something about these things. She wanted me to complain about every noise, every odor. But this was something that I simply could not do. I have always found it difficult to confront other people, and certainly, I felt unable to confront my downstairs neighbors about noises and odors that were well within normal range. The fact is, none of the problems that Joyce continually complained about seemed very bad to me.

But they seemed very bad to Joyce, and over time, she grew increasingly irritable at my refusal to complain to our neighbors. Because of that, we began to argue. At times, the arguments were very heated, and once, to escape the tension they generated, Joyce left the house completely, and walked to a nearby park, where she sat on a bench, wrapped in her coat, all alone in the snow, until I came for her, tugged her from the bench, and walked her back to the house. I can remember how she trembled beneath my arm as I led her home. There was a real sadness in her face, but there didn't seem to be much I could do to relieve it. I felt helpless. She would ask me if I loved her, and I would always reassure her, even though these reassurances never seemed to satisfy her.

When I think of those moments now, I think of my wife's need for love and my inability to show it in a way that would have been meaningful to her. I showed love by working, by striving, by tending to her every physical need, by moving toward a future which I expected to share with her. That was not what she needed, of course, but it was all that I could give. Thinking analytically, which is the way I tend to think, I saw myself as a dutiful husband, a provider of the essentials—food, clothing, shelter—the kind of man my father had been, which served as my only model for what a husband should be.

The fact that Joyce found it difficult to accept me as I was continued to plague our marriage in the coming months. It was a problem which our living conditions only made worse, and in the end, it became clear that these conditions, at least, had to be changed. The smell of our neighbor's cooking struck Joyce as rancid; the rustling of their pots and pans, intolerably disruptive. Both kept her from sleep, and so afflicted her nerves that she began to develop uncontrollable muscle spasms, which distressed her even more.

And so, approximately two months before Jeff's birth, in March of 1960, we moved to my parents' house in West Allis, Wisconsin.

But this move did very little to relieve Joyce's condition. She continued to suffer from long bouts of nausea; but now, a form of rigidity developed, one which none of the doctors who saw her was ever able to diagnose exactly. At times, her legs would lock tightly in place, and her whole body would grow rigid and begin to tremble. Her jaw would jerk to the right and take on a similarly frightening rigidity. During these strange seizures, her eyes would bulge like a frightened animal, and she would begin to salivate, literally frothing at the mouth.

Each time Joyce was taken by one of these seizures, I would take turns with my parents walking her around the dining room in an attempt to relieve the rigidity. Slowly, we would make our way around the dining room table, Joyce barely able to walk, but doing her best, while I held her up. This procedure very rarely worked, however. Because of that, a doctor would usually have to intervene, giving Joyce injections of barbiturates and morphine, which would finally relax her.

Joyce's doctor could find no medical reason for these sudden attacks. He suggested that they were rooted in Joyce's mental, rather than her physical, state. He said that they were probably tied to her being pregnant with her first baby. Still, something had to be done, and so he added phenobarbital to the list of medications that had already been prescribed.

This additional medication appeared to do little good, however, and, Joyce's emotional condition worsened. She became increasingly tense and irritable. She took offense quickly, and often seemed angry both with others, and at the generally harsh nature of her pregnancy.

During this period, I did what I thought I could do to keep Joyce comfortable, but at the same time, I realize now, I also left her alone with my parents quite often. I was a graduate student at Marquette University, studying for my master's in analytical chemistry. I was also working as a graduate assistant. As a result, I was away from home for much of the day, particularly during the last two months of her pregnancy. I would leave her at seven in the morning, and often not return until seven or eight in the evening. During those long, intervening hours, Joyce was forced to remain more or less housebound with my mother. She did not even have a driver's license. There was no relief, and if Joyce sometimes reacted with anger and resentment, it was not a reaction that anyone should find surprising. Despite all that, I was often baffled by what I saw as her inability to cope. The noise and odors that had driven her from our first apartment never seemed more than ordinary, and the situation at my parents' house appeared tolerable. Why was she so upset all the time? What was it that she found so dreadful?

As I learned later, it would have been impossible for me to have understood Joyce's situation. Her emotional makeup was totally different from mine. It was marked by peaks and valleys, highs and lows. Mine, as I have since discovered, was then, and still remains, a broad, flat plain.

To deal with the dips in her physical and emotional condition, Joyce continued taking various drugs. She would sometimes take as many as twenty-six pills a day. No doubt these helped to relieve some of her physical suffering, but for her emotional distress—the sense of helplessness and isolation that sometimes overwhelmed her—there appeared to be no relief. The irritability continued, and she grew more and more alienated from both me and my parents. I felt helpless to do anything about it. I found it difficult, as I have always found it difficult, to read the exact emotional state of another person, and during this time, I certainly found it difficult to read Joyce. So I floundered about, doing what I could, for the most part ineffectively. Joyce often lashed out at these awkward attempts to comfort her, a reaction that sometimes baffled me, since such anger was so different from my own way of handling things—the general passivity with which I have more often reacted to the ups and downs of life.

In any event, we never really came to terms with the conflicts of that first year. Because of that, I think that this first troubled experience laid the foundation for a longer, and even more troubled, marriage. In some sense, our relationship never recovered from the damage done to it at this early stage, never really improved.

Then, at the end of this long trial, my son was born.

I was at Marquette when he came. It was around four-forty-five in the afternoon, and I was working in the graduate-assistant office when the phone rang. It was my mother, telling me that my father had already taken Joyce to Deaconess Hospital, only a few blocks from Marquette.

I drove to the hospital immediately and discovered that Jeff had already been delivered. I went directly to Joyce's room and found her in bed, looking exhausted, of course, but also quite happy for the first time in many weeks. "You have a son," she said.

A few minutes later, I saw my son for the first time. He was in a small plastic bassinet, his body wrapped in a blue blanket. I could see him lying motionlessly on his side, eyes closed, sleeping quietly. I stared at him, astonished at how much he looked like me, how much I saw my own features, as if in miniature, in that tiny, pinkish face.

Joyce had said, "You have a son."

And so I did.

A son I would later name for myself.

Jeffrey Lionel Dahmer.

Jeffrey came home a few days later. One of his small legs was in a cast, a necessary orthopedic correction for a minor deformity, but otherwise, he was perfectly fine. Joyce held him gently in her arms, and as I drove all of us home, I could see his small eyes peering here and there, taking in the world for the first time.

I often think of him in that initial innocence. I imagine the shapes he must have seen, the blur of moving colors, and as I recall him in his infancy, I feel overwhelmed by a sense of helpless dread. I consider his eyes, blinking softly, and then I remember all the horrors they will later see. I dwell on the small, pink hands, and in my mind I watch them grow larger and darker as I think about all that they will later do, of how stained they will become with the blood of others. It is impossible to reconcile these visions, or to escape their sadness. They are like scenes from separate worlds, pages from different books, so that it is impossible to imagine how the end of my son's life could have sprung from the beginning of it.

For during those first few days, after we brought Jeff home, a happiness settled over us. The long ordeal of Joyce's pregnancy seemed over, a dreadful hardship which Jeff's birth had all but obliterated from our memories. For a time, we experienced that kind of joy which only parents know, the sense of life's being suddenly renewed and intensified. It was a happiness and lightheartedness that Joyce seemed to capture in the birth announcement she wrote and drew herself and sent to friends and relatives. On the front, she sketched a picture of a happy, smiling baby, surrounded by a swirl of pink bubbles, its tiny fist wrapped around a slide rule. Inside, Joyce had written a short poem:

> Chemistry has many phases
> With chemists in a fuss
> Well here's our little formula
> Patented by us!

But it was a happiness that lasted for only the shortest time. Within a few days of bringing Jeff home, problems began to develop once again.

First of all, there was the question of nursing. Something in the process seriously disturbed Joyce and made her irritable. She began to dread it terribly. My mother encouraged her to relax. She told Joyce that the initial pain and nervousness were natural, and that she would settle into the nursing routine after a short time. But Joyce never settled into nursing, never accepted it, and within a few days, she gave it up altogether. Her breasts were bound with a sheet in order to dry them up, and Jeff was henceforth fed by bottle.

As the days passed, other problems emerged. The cramped space of the bedroom we shared with Jeff was a source of strain and discontent. There were arguments with my mother, and after a while, these arguments settled into a permanent state of tension and bad feeling. Increasingly, Joyce withdrew from my mother, refusing to come down to the table to join the rest of us for dinner. Instead, she remained upstairs, alone in her bed, with Jeff sleeping quietly in the small bassinet a few feet away.

There were also arguments with me, disputes that seemed to have no solution. Often, Joyce would leave the house, and once, I found her nearly five blocks away, lying in a field of high grass, her body draped only in her nightgown.

By then, of course, I had become aware of Joyce's own childhood, of her father's alcoholism, of the long battle she had waged to overcome the domination and wildly explosive behavior he had imposed upon her and her entire family. But when I tried to analyze her situation, I always reached a wall I couldn't climb. What could I possibly do about her past? How could I make up for it? What could Joyce do about it, other than finally put it behind her? In my view, the point was to forget whatever fear or cruelty she'd experienced as a child, and to concentrate on the future. It seemed simple to me, clear and uncomplicated. You either overcame difficulties, or you were crushed by them.

My view, of course, was utterly one-dimensional. To that degree, it was also unreal, since it failed to recognize that Joyce was more complicated, and certainly more deeply wounded than I could imagine. She baffled me, and I felt helpless in dealing with her.

I couldn't understand where her fears and rages came from, and so I often avoided her, fleeing to my laboratory, where things were considerably less volatile, and where all reactions could be systematically controlled.

Because of that, Joyce often remained alone for long periods of time, isolated, in some sense helpless, while I was at work at Marquette, my life taking on a predictable and immensely comforting routine. I had tried to adjust my work schedule, of course, but all the same, and even when at home, I often occupied myself with course work and studying for exams. I was at home physically, but some other part of me was busy with other matters—with the future, as I saw it, the career which would, in the end, come to support my wife and child.

After a time, it became impossible to remain in my parents' house. There was just too much tension. And so, toward the beginning of September, when Jeff was four months old, we moved to Van Buren Street on the east side of Milwaukee.

The new residence was an old house that had been divided into six separate apartments. It wasn't exactly run-down, but it wasn't exactly modern, either. We had a one-bedroom apartment in the house, and it looked down on a working-class district of the city; a place for families, with small, inexpensive restaurants and ice cream parlors, the sort of place in which a struggling graduate student could locate his wife and child with a reasonable sense that they would be safe while he was away.

By this time, Jeff was babbling happily. He took great delight in sitting in his high chair while we fed him, energetically spitting his food out even as we struggled to make him eat. He seemed to take a fierce joy in this practice, laughing all the way down to the bottom of his stomach, his whole body shaking, as if seized in a frenzy of enjoyment.

For the next two years, we continued to live in this apartment while I worked at Marquette. Joyce remained at home with Jeff, seeing to his every need. She would take him for walks in the buggy, once as far as five miles to Marquette University to surprise me.

During all this time, our relationship was a mixture of good and bad times. It was not the period of constant tension it would later become. Joyce became more relaxed, as if she were beginning to adapt to her new "role" of wife and mother. To me, she seemed reasonably happy, reasonably content. As for Jeff, he remained a bubbly, likable child. He played continually in his "spider walker," scooting in all directions through the house and on the sidewalk on the side of the house, once hitting a crack, toppling over, bloodying his chin. I swept him into the house where Joyce applied first aid and we comforted him as he gradually stopped shaking and sucking in his breath in fright. He played with the usual stuffed toys, bunnies and dogs, with wooden blocks that he loved to stack carefully and then push over with a sudden, powerful thrust. In the fall, while in his playpen, he would sometimes gather up the surrounding leaves and begin to tear at them fiercely. Once, when I asked him what he was doing, he replied simply, "Ruputa leaves," which meant "ripping the leaves." Then he smiled.

In September of 1962, I was offered a graduate assistantship in the Ph.D. program at Iowa State University. I took it, and shortly after that, Joyce, Jeff, and I moved to the university's campus at Ames, Iowa.

We set up housekeeping in a small wooden house owned by the university and located at a place called Pammel Court. It was quite a bit smaller than our old apartment in Milwaukee, and it was surrounded by similar structures, along with an assortment of Quonset huts that had been constructed during the Second World War.

The university offer had included a generous stipend, and both Joyce and I saw the move as a step up, a move we were both making toward a better future.

Once in the new house, I quickly got into my new work at the university. At first I had a teaching assistantship, but after that I got a research assistantship, a post that was much more to my liking. In the new work, I would not be required to deal with students. Instead, I would be working with chemicals and lab equipment, surrounded by analytical instruments in an environment that was nearly free of contact with students. As such, it was a welcome change from the sort of work I'd been doing. Although I enjoyed working with students, the lab offered different challenges, and I soon began to think of it as the place where I really flourished. In the lab, the iron-clad laws of science governed an otherwise chaotic world of actions and reactions. In the world at large, and particularly regarding my relationship with Joyce, things were more obscure and complicated. It was often hard for me to know exactly where I stood, or what I should do at any particular moment. The lab, on the other hand, was a place where I felt safe in my judgments, secure in my expertise. Outside it, I felt far less certain of myself, far less able to perceive things correctly. As a result, I stayed at the lab not only because there was a great deal of work, but because I felt relief and comfort in the fact that I could adequately understand what went on there, that I understood the laws that governed things.

Meanwhile, Joyce remained at home at Pammel Court. We had found the house in a very unwholesome state when we'd arrived, and Joyce had resentfully knuckled down to the task of doing far more cleaning and scrubbing than she'd anticipated. Once again, she found herself more or less locked away at home, while I spent my days, and now a good deal of my nights, at work in the laboratory.

As a result, her emotional state began to deteriorate. A recurrent dream plagued her, one in which she was continually being chased by a large black bear. She sometimes screamed in her sleep. At times I would try to calm her, making the typical suggestions of an analytic mind, recommending that she walk around a bit, or drink a glass of warm milk, but never moving to engage the actual dream, or the roots from which it sprang.

Predictably, our arguments became more heated, and at times, physical. On some occasions, when I would fight back vigorously, Joyce would seize a kitchen knife and make jabbing motions. In response, I would go into another room, or leave the house altogether.

But if Joyce and I were having a great deal of trouble with each other, we were also having problems with Jeff. Several times during those years, he fell victim to various infections. Almost every week seemed to bring another round of illness. He often contracted ear and throat infections which would keep him crying through the night. Over and over, he was taken to the university clinic for injections, and after a time, his little buttocks were covered with injection lumps, and he began to lash out at the nurses and doctors who labored to treat him.

But there were good times, too, times when Jeff was healthy and vigorous and full of fun. We went to parades and festivals, and Ames had its own small zoo, which we occasionally visited. I set up a swing set beside our house, and made a sandbox for Jeff to play in when the weather was such that he could stay outdoors.

Through it all, Jeff remained a happy, ebullient child. When I arrived at home for supper, he would come rushing to me and jump into my arms. He was eager and expressive, and he loved to play and to be read to in the evening. He played with large blocks now, and rode a small tricycle. Even more, he loved for me to take him riding on a bicycle, his body seated on the chrome handlebars.

On one of these rides, Jeff suddenly demanded that I stop immediately. He was quite excited, his eyes very wide as he fixed them on something I could not make out.

When I brought the bicycle to a halt, he pointed up ahead and to the right.

"Look," he said, "look at that."

"What?" I asked, still unable to see what he was pointing at.

"It's right there," Jeff cried.

I looked more closely in the direction he indicated, and saw a small mound that looked like little more than a clump of dirt. When I drew closer, I saw that it was a nighthawk that had fallen from its nest and now lay helplessly on the hard pavement. We parked the bike and went closer. At first, we didn't know what to do, but at Jeff's urging, I picked it up and together we took it home. Over the next few weeks we nursed it to health, feeding it a mixture of milk and corn syrup which we served by means of a baby bottle. After a time, the bird took solid food, bread, and finally small bits of hamburger. It grew larger and larger, and we finally took it outside to release it. It was a bright spring day, and I can still remember how green everything looked.

I cradled the bird in my cupped hand, lifted it into the air, then opened my hand and let it go. As it spread its wings and rose into the air, we, all of us—Joyce, Jeff, and myself—felt a wonderful delight. Jeff's eyes were wide and gleaming. It may have been the single, happiest moment of his life.

New graduate-school arrivals Jeff, Joyce, and Lionel, Iowa State University, 1962

CHAPTER TWO

When I was a little boy, I developed an obsession. Slowly, over time, I became fixated upon, in a sense, hypnotized by, the physical presence of fire. There was an old man who lived only three or four houses down from my childhood home. He had a wooden leg, and smoked a pipe. When he wanted to smoke his pipe, he struck the necessary match on his wooden leg. As a child, I saw him do it many times, and I think that perhaps my early obsession with fire stemmed from this single, curious, and often-repeated event.

For whatever cause, and in response to whatever developing obsession, my fixation grew over the years. For a time, I had a large matchbook collection. Still later, I began the practice of stealing matches. I'd snatch them from wherever I found them, lying on a table, or tucked away in a drawer. Then I'd sneak away to some deserted spot and strike them one by one and gaze intently, as if transfixed by the dancing flames.

As it remained in its early stages, my father never knew of my fixation with fire. Holding down two jobs,

27

one as a high-school math teacher and the other as a barber, he was a busy man. He knew only what most fathers know about their children. He knew when they were sick, when they'd been physically hurt, and when they'd triumphed or failed in some important matter.

My father, of course, did not know anything of my inner life. He did not know, for example, that at times during the school day, I began experiencing new and mysterious (to me) sensations as I climbed the jungle gym or the parallel bars, or as I rubbed up against bathroom stalls. He did not know that I later fantasized about ample, buxom women. These are the sorts of things, of course, that fathers rarely know about their growing sons, the private world of their developing sexual needs, the twists they take as they find ways of satisfying them.

Nevertheless, my father was very involved in his role as parent, particularly so, given the general approach to fatherhood at the time, which was to be somewhat distant, a figure whose primary function was to provide for the necessities and maintain discipline. He made time for me. He helped me with my homework and attended all the necessary parent-teacher conferences at my school. He played catch with me, took me swimming, sledding, and camping. At Christmas he made sure I visited Santa at the local department store. He was, then, a good father, as caring and concerned as any son could wish.

But there were things he didn't know, and one of them was that his son had begun to drift, helplessly and innocently drift, toward a fixation which had, in its most dreadful form, the potential for a vast and unfathomable destruction.

And so, I continued with my obsession. It grew larger, and began to include a fascination with bombs, with the making of explosives. Still, it was fire that haunted me until, while indulging my obsession one summer afternoon, I very nearly burned down a neighbor's garage.

Then, at last, my father learned that there were dangerous impulses in me, that somewhere, without knowing why or how, a dark pathway had been dug into my brain.

What followed was a stern lecture on the dangers of fire, on its destructive power, on how careful I had to be in the future to control an interest which, if uncontrolled, would inevitably lead to acts of enormous harm.

I remember listening to my father's severe warning. I remember thinking that I had gone astray, that I had somehow picked up a fascination that could have terrible consequences. More than anything, I remember thinking that it was an interest which I absolutely had to channel and control, even if it took every ounce of will.

When I remember my father's reaction to my obsession with fire, I see it as incredibly old-fashioned. It was nothing more than a stern rebuke, a warning that was based upon my father's own confident notion that my fascination with fire was one I could control by means of my will alone. It would never have occurred to him that such a fascination might attach itself to my sexuality, that it might hook on to that relentlessly driving engine, and that if it did, my will would be crushed beneath it like a small twig beneath a roaring train. His naïveté protected him from such dark imaginings.

I think my naïveté protected me, as well, from an early uneasiness about what might have been developing in my son.

In the late fall of 1964, when Jeff was four years old, and we were still living at Pammel Court, I noticed a smell which very clearly came from beneath the house. I took a flashlight and a plastic bucket and crawled under the house to find whatever it was that was generating such an unbearable odor. A few minutes later I located a large pile of bones, the remains of various small rodents which had probably been killed by the civets that populated the general area. It was the foul smell of the civets, a close relative of the skunk, that had invaded the house. They had used the area under our house as a place for devouring the small creatures they preyed upon at night.

Within a few minutes, I'd gathered up all the small animal remains I could find. It was a varied assortment of bones, white, dry, and completely fleshless, since they had been picked clean by the civets.

Joyce and Jeff were waiting for me as I came out from under the house. Once on my feet again, I set the bucket down and began to talk to Joyce. I was still talking to her a few minutes later when I glanced down and saw Jeff as he sat on the ground only a few feet away. He had taken a great many of the bones from the bucket and was staring at them intently. From time to time, he would pick a few of them up, then let them fall with a brittle, crackling sound that seemed to fascinate him. Over and over, he would pick up a fistful of bones, then let them drop back into the pile that remained on the bare ground.

I went over to him, and as I bent down to gather up the bones and throw them away, Jeff released another small cluster of bones and let them clatter to the ground. He seemed oddly thrilled by the sound they made. "Like fiddlesticks," he said. Then he laughed and walked away.

In the last few years, I have often thought of my son as he looked that afternoon, his small hands dug deep into a pile of bones. I can no longer view it simply as a childish episode, a passing fascination. It may have been nothing more than that, but now I have to see it in a different way, in a more sinister and macabre light. It was once nothing more than a rather sweet memory of my little boy, but now it has the foretaste of his doom, and comes to me, as it often does, on the thin edge of a chill.

This same sense of something dark and shadowy, of a malicious force growing in my son, now colors almost every memory I have of his childhood. In a sense, his childhood no longer exists. Everything is now a part of what he did as a man. Because of that, I can no longer distinguish the ordinary from the forbidding—trivial events from ones loaded with foreboding. When he was four, and pointed to his belly button and asked what would happen if someone cut it out, was that merely an ordinary question from a child who had begun to explore his own body, or was it a sign of something morbid already growing in his mind? When, at six, Jeff broke several windows out in an old, abandoned building, was that only a typical boyhood prank, or was it the early signal of a dark and impulsive destructiveness? When we went fishing, and he seemed captivated by the gutted fish, staring intently at the brightly colored entrails, was that a child's natural curiosity, or was it a harbinger of the horror that was later to be found in Apartment 213?

In me, of course, an early obsession with fire had led to nothing more unusual than chemistry, to a lifelong work in scientific research. Jeff's momentary fascination with bones might just as easily have pointed to an early interest that might have led eventually to medicine or medical research. It might have led to orthopedics or anatomical drawing or sculpture. It might simply have led to taxidermy. Or, more likely, it might have pointed to absolutely nothing, and been forgotten.

But now, I will never be able to forget it. Now, it is an early suggestion, whether actual or not, of a subtle direction in my son's thought.

At the time, however, I hardly thought of it at all. And so, to the extent that I gave Jeff any early guidance, at least as far as his future interests might be, it was toward the sciences, particularly chemistry.

Not long after I'd discarded the animal remains I'd found beneath our house, I took Jeff to my chemistry laboratory for the first time. We walked from home, his hand in mine as we moved down the narrow dirt road that led from our house to the university's metallurgy building.

My lab was on the third floor, at the end of a long corridor. It was on a weekend, and so, for the most part, Jeff and I had the run of the laboratory. For the next hour, I showed Jeff as much as I could of my work, introducing him to what, for me, were the fascinations of chemistry. I did the acid-base litmus test, and Jeff watched attentively as the paper turned either red or blue. He stared wonderingly as a beaker of phenolphthalein turned dark pink when I introduced ammonia into the solution. The steady click of the Geiger counter briefly amused him.

But at the same time, he asked no questions, and seemed more or less indifferent to the laboratory atmosphere. It was a day's outing, nothing more, and when it was over, he appeared no more interested in the mechanics of science than he might have been in a light show or a fireworks display. He was a child enjoying the company of his father, and when our time in the lab was over and we strolled back down the dirt road toward home, he bounced along beside me with the same energy and playfulness that he'd shown as we'd walked to the lab earlier in the day. There was no suggestion that he'd developed even the most fleeting interest in anything I'd shown him. Nothing in the vast array of laboratory equipment, the walls of bottled chemicals, the glittering cabinets filled with tubes and vials and beakers, nothing in all that had managed to captivate him with anything like the power of old bones like fiddlesticks.

During the next year, while I struggled to finish my Ph.D., I watched Jeff grow larger and more animated. He remained playful, but his play had begun to take on a definite pattern. He didn't care for any form of competition, and shunned games that involved physical contact. He didn't engage in scuffling or other forms of childhood wrestling. Instead, he preferred games whose rules were highly defined and nonconfrontational, games full of repetitive actions, particularly those that were generally based on themes of stalking and concealment, games like hide-and-seek, kick the can, and ghost in the graveyard.

Sometimes, when I would come home from the lab to grab a quick supper before returning to it, I would see Jeff crouching behind a tree or hiding behind bushes. At those moments, he seemed totally absorbed, so I rarely made the effort to break his concentration by calling to him or waving as I walked into the house. Instead, I let him go, had my supper, and left seconds later, bent upon my own obsession, which was, perhaps, no less intense than his.

Once at the lab, I became absorbed in my own work. I was never a great student. What others got quickly, took me much longer. I was a plodder, a plugger, a hard worker. For me, anything less than an all-out effort would mean failure. Others had flashes of creative brilliance, of sudden illumination, but I had only the power of my own will.

During our time at Pammel Court, I exercised that will to the fullest. My Ph.D. work became, quite literally, my life. I thought of almost nothing else. Inevitably then, other parts of my life began to blur. Joyce blurred. And so did Jeff.

I saw him in glimpses, a boy shooting around the room or eating at the dinner table. I felt him in snatches, a quick hug on the way in or out. I spoke to him in brief hellos, in good-byes tossed over my shoulder as I left the room. The Ph.D. loomed before me like an enormous mountain. Everything else seemed small.

But Jeff was not small. He was getting bigger every day. Still, I barely saw him grow, barely glimpsed the changes that were creeping over him. And so, it was not until Jeff suddenly became ill that I was brought to a full stop.

The illnesses that had plagued Jeff during the early years of his life had gone away as he'd grown older. He seemed healthy and robust, a normal kid in every way. Then, suddenly, he was stricken.

One day in the spring of 1964, Jeff began to complain about an area of tenderness in his groin area. This tenderness worsened, and a small bulge appeared in his scrotum. We took him to the doctor right away, and he was subsequently diagnosed as suffering from a double hernia. The doctor explained that the hernia was the result of a birth defect, and that surgery was necessary to correct the problem.

Surgery was scheduled for the following week, and while Joyce and I stood by, Jeff selected the ragged, floppy-eared dog he'd slept with since the age of two as the stuffed animal he wished to accompany him to the hospital.

The operation was performed shortly after, and when it was over, Jeff was taken to his room, where he remained sedated for several hours. When he awoke, of course, it was to a great deal of pain. So much pain, I learned later, that he had asked Joyce if the doctors had cut off his penis.

He remained in the hospital for several days, and even after he'd returned home, his recovery seemed to move forward slowly. For long hours, he remained on the sofa in the living room, his body wrapped in a large, checkered bathrobe. During that period, he moved slowly, ponderously, like an old man. The ebullience which had marked his childhood, his buoyancy and energy drained away.

During any period of recovery, of course, a certain flattening of mood could be expected. But in Jeff, this flattening began to take on a sense of something permanent. He seemed smaller, somehow more vulnerable, perhaps even sadder than at any time before.

By the fall of 1966, when our time at Pammel Court was coming to an end, this strange and subtle inner darkening began to appear almost physically. His hair, which had once been so light, grew steadily darker, along with the deeper shading of his eyes. More than anything, he seemed to grow more inward, sitting quietly for long periods, hardly stirring, his face oddly motionless. Now, when I look at photographs of my son at this age, I can't help but wonder if strange shapes were already forming in his mind, odd notions that he himself could not understand, vague fantasies that might have frightened even him, but which he could not keep at bay. In the pictures, I can see only a kid playing in the yard or sitting silently with his dog, but I wonder if, even as he did those things, he was already sinking into a world that was invisible to me. I wonder if the world of monsters which other children were beginning to cast aside, was, in my son, growing larger and more hideously populated with each passing day.

As for me, I saw only a quiet little boy, who, at least after we left Pammel Court, appeared more withdrawn than before, more inward, less likely to flash his quick warm smile. It is possible that I didn't see anything more than that because I was rushing past my son too quickly. Sometimes, almost from the corner of my eyes, I would glimpse my son as he sat on the sofa, staring blankly at the flickering television. I can't remember the look on his face or recall to any degree the light in his eyes. More seriously, I can't recall noticing that some earlier light was slowly going out. And so I wasn't there to see him as he began to sink into himself. I wasn't there to sense, even if I could have sensed it, that he might be drifting toward that unimaginable realm of fantasy and isolation that it would take me nearly thirty years to recognize. And yet, it may have been happening even then, while I gulped down my dinner and bolted past him for the door, comforted by the notion that I was the only member of our family who was going out into the night.

I received my Ph.D. in October of 1966, and a month later, I took my first job as a research chemist for a large chemical company in the Akron, Ohio, area. We found a small house in Doylestown, a colonial twinplex with four white columns on the front, the largest house we'd ever lived in.

Joyce was pregnant again, a pregnancy that exhibited the same problems as her first. Noise was bothering her again, and she was often nervous, sleepless, and irritable. She took two to three Equanil a day to help with her condition. But they did not seem to help very much, and so the dosage was increased to three to five tablets a day. Even this increase did not ameliorate her general condition, however. The nervousness continued, and as it did, Joyce became more withdrawn until, by the time of David's birth, in December of 1966, we hardly had any social life at all.

During this time, of course, I spent most of my time at work at my new job. In the lab, I once again found a wonderful comfort and assurance in knowing the properties of things, how they could be manipulated in predictable patterns. It provided a great relief from the chaos I found at home, the volatility of Joyce's emotions, the continual shifts within her mood. The lab was a haven from those storms, and I probably worked even longer hours because of that.

As for Jeff, he had started first grade at Hazel Harvey Elementary School in Doylestown, but he had done so reluctantly. A strange fear had begun to creep into his personality, a dread of others that was combined with a general lack of self-confidence. It was as if he had come to expect that other people might harm him in some way, and so he wanted to stay clear of them.

Without doubt, the move from Pammel Court had darkened Jeff's mood considerably. Perhaps it was the fact that we'd found it necessary to leave his cat behind, or perhaps it was the fact that he was already developing a reluctance to change, a need to feel the assurance of familiar places. Certainly, the prospect of going to school frightened and unnerved him. He had taken on the shyness that would later become a permanent aspect of his character. His posture had become more rigid, so that he stood very erect, as if at attention, his fingers pressed tightly against the sides of his legs.

On the morning of his first scheduled school day, I remember the terror that swept into his face. He appeared nearly speechless, his features frozen. The little boy who'd once seemed so happy and self-assured had disappeared. He had been replaced by someone else, a different person, now deeply shy, distant, nearly uncommunicative.

It was this child who entered Hazel Harvey Elementary School in the fall of 1966. It was not surprising then that a month later, when I met with Jeff's first-grade teacher, her description of my son was of this new person. Mrs. Allard, an extremely empathetic teacher, told me that Jeff had impressed her as being inordinately shy and reclusive. He had been polite and had followed all her instructions, but he had given the impression of a profound unhappiness. He had not interacted with the other children. Although he had done the work assigned to him, he had done it without interest, merely as a task that had to be completed. He had not been able to engage in conversation with other children. He had not responded to their casual approaches, nor made any approaches of his own. On the playground, he'd kept to himself, merely pacing about the schoolyard, doing what she described as "nothing."

Of course, to me, all of this was rooted in the fact that we had suddenly moved Jeff to a different house, a different neighborhood, even a different state. I'd heard other stories of children who'd been briefly disoriented by being abruptly taken from familiar settings and plopped down in completely unfamiliar ones. The somberness I saw in his manner struck me as no more than a normal reaction. My son, it seemed to me, was not very good at adapting to new circumstances, but this was a flaw that could hardly be seen as fatal.

Still, Jeff's shyness and reclusiveness were serious

enough to require some kind of action. As for the teacher, in concluding our meeting, she assured me that she would do all she could to bring Jeff out a bit, integrate him into the school community.

On the way home that evening, I recalled my own early shyness. It seemed to me that Jeff's behavior during the preceding weeks had been more or less the same as mine had been on those occasions when I'd suddenly found myself thrust into unfamiliar surroundings. As a boy, I'd been horribly shy, just as he was. Each year, I'd dreaded moving up to the next grade, even when that move would not mean any change in school buildings, and despite the fact that I would still be surrounded by children I already knew. It was as if some element of my character yearned for complete predictability, for rigid structure. Change, whether good or bad, was something fearful to me, something to be avoided. Awkward and insecure, plagued by a grave sense of my own inadequacy, as a child I had conceived of the world as something hostile and suspicious, a place that sometimes confused me, and which, because of that, I had come to regard with a sense of grave uneasiness.

It was as if I could not exactly figure out the social connections that others seemed to understand immediately. The subtleties of social life were beyond my grasp. When children liked me, I did not know why. When they disliked me, I did not know why. Nor could I formulate a plan for winning their affection. I simply didn't know how things worked with other people. There seemed to be a certain randomness and unpredictability in their attitudes and actions. And try as I might, I couldn't find a way to make other people seem less strange and unknowable. Because of that, the social world seemed vague and threatening. And so, as a boy, I had approached it with a great lack of confidence, even dread.

As I later observed Jeff, noting his fear of school, his awkwardness and lack of friends, it struck me that he had probably inherited this same dread. Because I had experienced it before him, I sympathized with it and felt that I understood it. In the same sense, be-cause I had become familiar with this dread, it had become less dreadful, and over the years I had been able to create a life that seemed to function more or less like any other. I had managed to get an educa-tion. I had a family and held down a job. Despite the dread, the feelings of inferiority, the terrible shyness, all the insecurities that had afflicted me as a boy and which still lingered into adulthood—despite all of those things—I was living what I and others took to be a normal life. And so, when I saw these same char-acteristics as they emerged in Jeff, they did not appear to me as anything particularly dangerous or frighten-ing. I had been plagued by the same feelings that were plaguing him, but I had learned to cope with them, and finally, to overcome them. Since, over the years I had learned to live with them, I saw no reason why my son could not learn to live with them, too.

I realize now that I was wrong, that Jeff's boyhood condition was far graver than mine had ever been. For while I had suffered from shyness, Jeff had begun to suffer from a near total isolation. While I had known the power of an odd fascination, Jeff had begun to move into the grip of a profound perversity. Now, when I gaze at the photographs of him from that time, I wonder at all that must have been forming behind his eyes. I also wonder if there were any visible signs of it. Could I have glimpsed it, had I been more watchful? Would I have recognized what it was I glimpsed, or would I have quickly filed it under the generic label of "childhood trouble" and let it go, hoping that adulthood would bring a cure for whatever it was I sensed, but could not clearly understand. Was there any means by which I might have pulled my son from the jaws that were beginning to devour him?

When I ask myself these questions, a memory invariably returns to me. Not long after we left Pammel Court, as I drove down the street coming home from work, I saw Jeff alone at the edge of the lawn. It had been raining, and he was dressed in a winter jacket and stocking cap. As I neared him, I could see that he was flailing about, his arms in the air, his dog, Frisky, barking loudly as she circled him wildly. For a moment, they seemed to be playing together, but as I pulled into the driveway, I could see that Jeff had become mired in mud at the edge of the lawn, and was trying desperately to extricate himself. He was sobbing loudly, huge tears cascading down his face, and I could see that his fear of being pulled down or swallowed up by the earth had sent him into a full-scale panic.

I ran to him as fast as I could, snatched him from the mud, and lifted him into my arms. I could see his face light up with a great joy and sense of rescue. He was smiling and crying at the same time, his whole being flooded with the immense relief that someone, at last, had seen his distress and had finally pulled him from the sucking earth. He leaned toward me, his arms wrapped tightly around my neck, and brought his face very close to mine. I can still remember the sweetness of his breath, the immense gratitude I could see in his eyes.

I know now what my son must have felt at that moment. His father had rescued him from what had seemed a terrible fate, and perhaps, in his young mind, Jeff might have believed that I would always be able to see his peril and snatch him from it.

But the part of Jeff that was most in danger was invisible to me. I could see only those aspects of his character that he chose to show, which resembled some of my own characteristics—the shyness, the general tone of acceptance, the tendency to withdraw from conflict. I suppose, like most fathers, I even took some comfort, perhaps even a bit of pride, in thinking that my son was a bit like me.

We moved again when Jeff was seven, this time to a rented house in Barberton. I assumed that he would deal with it in his own way. It would disorient him again, but it seemed to me that learning to deal with change was a lesson in itself. Change, after all, was a part of life. Something no one could avoid. In being moved yet again, Jeff was only being taught another lesson in learning to adapt.

By then, of course, Jeff was already having to adapt to more than a new location. Several months before, Joyce had given birth to our second son, David.

Unlike Jeff, David had had a difficult first few months. He had suffered from colic, and kept Joyce and me up night after night. This increased the tension that had been steadily building between the two of us, and everything became considerably more difficult.

This problem was made worse by the fact that Joyce had gone into an acute depression. She was extremely irritable, and spent much of her time in bed. With Joyce in such a condition, most of the household and child-rearing duties fell to me. Because of this, I attended worship services with Jeff less and less frequently, until I finally rationalized that I could be spiritually fulfilled by reading at home. Some of these duties, however, were quite pleasant, and I particularly remember the two mile walks I took with Jeff and his dog Frisky to a farm to buy eggs, returning to cook breakfast for all of us. Then, on Saturday afternoons, Jeff and I drove to nearby Barberton, Ohio, for our regular chocolate ice cream sodas, a habit carried over from Ames, Iowa.

My relationship with Joyce was less pleasant, however. Although we argued quite a bit, our arguments remained within what might be called the normal limits. We did not scream at each other. We did not throw things. We fought, then retired from the field. But there were also good times interspersed among the bad, so it was hard for me to tell that our marriage was beginning to unravel.

Dave was five months old when we moved to Barberton. It was in April of 1967, and Dave slept in Joyce's arms as we drove to our new house. As for Jeff, he sat in the backseat, rather blank, neither excited nor particularly frightened, as if his emotional range had begun to narrow. The intensity of his earlier feelings had leveled off. He seemed more passive, his attitude taking on the strange resignation that would soon become a central feature of his character.

Once in Barberton, I remember Jeff and Frisky playing in the backyard of the new house, Jeff dressed in blue jeans and a striped T-shirt. In flashes, he appeared to return to the carefree and energetic behavior I remembered from Pammel Court. Not long after moving into our new house, he made acquaintance with a young boy who lived in the house behind us. His name was Lee, and he and Jeff played together in the afternoon. In October, they went trick-or-treating together. Joyce served them a "witch's brew" of orange sherbet and ginger ale, and then the two set out together, marching from house to house throughout the neighborhood, both of them dressed as devils. Before leaving, the two boys stood together for a photograph, both of them smiling brightly in their devil costumes.

In the picture, Jeff is on the left, and there is no suggestion that within a few years, his life would veer radically away from the life of that other little boy. He seems relaxed, happy, totally at ease with his newfound friend.

I have looked at this picture many times, and there is not the slightest hint that in only a few years my son would find it so difficult to confront another human being that he would lie in wait for a jogger he'd found attractive, lie in wait in the bushes, with a baseball bat in his hand, with the intent of using it to knock out the jogger so that he could "lie down with him," as he later said—lie down with an unconscious body. In the photograph, there is not a hint that he was becoming so afraid of other people, so intimidated by their presence, that in order for him to have contact with them, they needed to be dead.

Even now, when I think of all that has happened since that time, I wonder if it might have been possible to stop his course. Clearly, there were flashes of affection, when something kind and childlike burst through the enveloping mask of distance and withdrawal. There was even at least one instance, when Jeff was in the third grade, when he actually reached out to someone beyond the family circle.

She was an assistant teacher, and I don't know the exact nature of their relationship, only that Jeff developed a certain fondness for her. Perhaps she had befriended him in some small way. Perhaps she had tried to break through an isolation and sense of trouble that she could see better than either Joyce or I could. Perhaps it was no more than a smile or a touch that she had casually extended which had struck Jeff as something wonderful and delicious.

Years later, when I asked Jeff why he'd come to like this particular woman, he responded with little more than a verbal shrug. "She was nice to me, I guess," he answered in the lifeless monotone that had become his voice by then. He did not remember her name, nor anything she had done that had caused him to like her more than any other teacher. It was as if she'd been no more than a passing shadow, mildly pleasant, but of no importance.

And so I will never know what it was in this

woman that made Jeff respond to her. I only know that he did respond, did reach out, did make a small, awkward gesture toward another human being.

It was nothing more than a child's gift, a bowl of tadpoles which Jeff had caught in a stream in the field behind U. L. Light School, where Jeff, Frisky, and I regularly roamed and shot basketballs on Saturdays and sometimes after work. He gave them to her innocently, as an expression of his affection. Later, however, he found out that the teaching assistant had given these same tadpoles to Lee. In revenge, Jeff later sneaked into Lee's garage, found the bowl of tadpoles, and poured motor oil into their water, killing them.

To my knowledge, this was Jeff's first act of violence. One of the guide wires that had held him in check suddenly slipped from its securing bolt, and for a fleeting moment, the darker Jeff, the one who was growing larger and larger as my son grew up, suddenly emerged in the form of a little boy pouring motor oil into a bowl of tadpoles.

In the years to come, that darker side would grow more powerful in my son, until it finally attached itself to his budding sexuality, and after that, entirely consumed him.

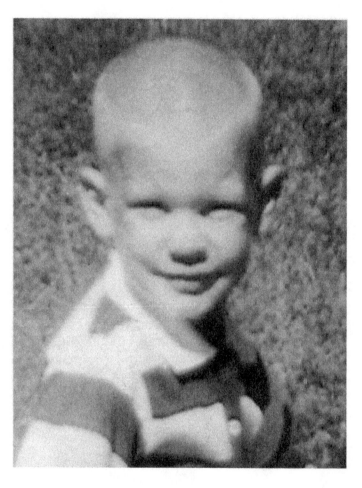

Jeff, comfortable in Grandma and Grandpa Dahmer's old-fashioned backyard, West Allis, Wisconsin, 1964

CHAPTER THREE

I remember my first sexual fantasy. I was probably around ten years old at the time, and I had taken to reading *Li'l Abner* in the comics. In reading it, I had become fixated on the robust and buxom women who appeared in the strip. In my fantasy, I dreamed of being taken by one of them in some kind of sexual embrace. It wasn't sex, exactly, but I know that it was rooted in sex, and that comic-book characters, rather than real people, were the first genuine objects of my emerging sexual desire.

In later years, all of that would change, and my fantasies would begin to move toward more predictable objects of desire, women of great beauty whom I saw in magazines, or famous singers and movie stars. My fantasy life would become, for lack of a better word, "normal," and I would dream of the blond girl who lived down the street, my sexuality gradually taking on those richer and more mature aspects that finally allow it to be linked to love.

Sometimes, when I think of Jeff at nine or ten, I wonder if he had begun to move toward some fantasy that came from nowhere and slowly began to take up permanent residence in his mind. In a psychiatric evaluation which I later read, my son claimed to have had his first sexual fantasies at around fourteen, but I saw changes in Jeff long before he reached that age, and it is hard for me to believe that dark notions, regardless of how vague and formless, were not already shaping in his mind.

For one thing, his posture, and the general way in which he carried himself, changed radically during the years between his tenth and fifteenth years. The loose-limbed boy disappeared, and was replaced by a strangely rigid and inflexible figure. He looked continually tense, his body very straight. When he walked, his legs appeared to lock at the knee. This caused his legs to stiffen so much that his feet seemed to scrape across the ground, as if he were dragging them along rather than being carried by them.

He grew increasingly shy during this time, as well, and when approached by other people, he would become very tense. Often, he would grab a small stick or a piece of grass and begin winding it nervously around his fingers. It was as if he could not confront another person without holding onto something, a mooring, perhaps, or a weapon.

More and more, he remained at home, alone in his room or staring at television. His face was often blank, and he gave the more or less permanent impression of someone who could do nothing but mope around, purposeless and disengaged.

Many times, I tried to pull him from what I saw as the quagmire of his own inactivity, only to discover that his interests remained limited and desultory, that he did not stick with things for very long. At various times, he tried both soccer and tennis, but eventually gave them up.

We lived in a large wooded area at this time, and so, after tennis and soccer had failed to engage Jeff, I decided that he might prefer a more solitary pastime. I bought him a professional-level bow and arrow, set up a target in one of the broad open fields, and taught him how to shoot. Initially, he appeared quite interested in the sport, and we would often go target-shooting together. But once again, in what had become a predictable pattern, he quickly lost interest, and the bow and arrow were tucked into the back corner of his closet while Jeff lay sprawled on his bed or walked aimlessly about the house.

By the time he was twelve, Jeff had given up most of what young boys continued to pursue during their preadolescence. He cared very little for sports, even less for boyhood academic pursuits like chemistry or biology sets. Although a Boy Scout trip to New Mexico appeared to have intrigued him, he made no effort to stay in the Scouts once he returned home.

By the time he reached fifteen, he had abandoned

almost everything to which I had introduced him. He appeared shy, as always, but even less self-confident.

During this time, I found that to some extent I could identify with Jeff's situation. I could recognize certain features of my own boyhood in what I saw him going through. I had sometimes felt left out, particularly when some of my friends began to go out on dates. Like Jeff, I appeared quite introverted.

But unlike me, Jeff seemed unable to pursue even the most casual interests. He never read anything other than the books assigned in school, and science fiction and Alfred Hitchcock's book called *Horror Stories for Children.* Although he participated in the school band for a time, he showed no interest in music, no interest in art. Even worse, he showed no interest in other people. And even though he considered a neighborhood boy, Greg, as his closest friend until they drifted apart at age fifteen, he never developed relationships with his fellow schoolmates.

Because of all this, it was easy for me to see my own preadolescence as very similar to Jeff's, and it struck me that at one point in my boyhood I had hit upon something that had helped me to come out of my shyness by building up my self-confidence. It was possible, I thought at the time, that the strategy might work for Jeff, as well.

I suggested bodybuilding. I thought if he could get a better image of himself physically, then perhaps he might become less isolated socially. It had worked for me to a great extent, and I hoped that it would work for him.

I mentioned bodybuilding to Jeff one afternoon, and he took an immediate interest. A few days later, I came home with a Bullworker, for isometric exercises, and showed him how to use it. As he listened to me give my instructions, he seemed more engaged than I had seen him in a long time.

During the next few weeks, I often caught glimpses of Jeff spread out on the floor of his room, intently at work with the Bullworker I had bought him. At other times, the door would be closed, but I could hear Jeff breathing loudly behind it as he pumped furiously at his newfound toy.

Although the Bullworker occupied Jeff for a good year and afforded him a well-developed sixteen-year-old upper body, it, too, was set aside, joining the tennis racket, the soccer ball, and the bow and arrow in Jeff's unlighted closet.

Now, when I think of these discarded things, they take on a deep metaphorical significance for me. They are the small, ultimately ineffectual offerings I made in the hope of steering my son toward a normal life. When I remember them, I see them almost as artifacts of a blasted life, curiosities united by nothing more than a deep, enduring sadness. For the Jeff who might have been engaged by such things was already gone.

And so, during the next few years, instead of pursuing any of the interests and activities which I had naively offered him, my son would find interests of his own. Steadily, and without my knowing it, his fascination with bones would develop into a full-blown adolescent obsession. As I first learned at the trial in February of 1992, he would begin to roam the nearby streets of our neighborhood, always on his bike, but further equipped with a supply of plastic garbage bags with which he could retrieve the remains of animals he found along his way. He would gather together these animal remains and create his own private cemetery. He would strip the flesh from the bodies of these putrescent road kills and even mount a dog's head on a stake.

As I heard about these activities for the first time at the trial, I wondered why someone hadn't mentioned even one of these incidents to me. And even more puzzling, why hadn't I seen evidence of these things? Many months after the trial, I learned that the "cemetery" had been on a small mounded area in the woods on a neighbor's property across the road, and that the dog's head on a stake had been in a secluded area of woods southwest of our property, two neighbors away.

As a person Jeff would grow more passive, more solitary, more inexpressibly isolated. He would have neither male nor female friends. He would form no relationships other than the most casual and convenient. In the world outside his mind, everything would become increasingly dull and flat, his conversation narrowing to the practice of answering questions with barely audible one-word responses. The boy who sat across from me at the dinner table, his face now adorned with glasses, his eyes dull, his mouth set in a motionless rigidity, was drifting into a nightmare world of unimaginable fantasies.

In the coming years, those fantasies would begin to overwhelm him. He would be assailed by visions of murder and dismemberment. The dead in their stillness would become the primary objects of his growing sexual desire. More and more, as a teenager, his inability to speak about such strange and unsettling notions would sever his connections to the world outside himself.

But all that I really noticed during those years of my son's adolescence was his increasing inwardness and disconnection. He did only what he had to do in school, and exhibited neither interests nor ambitions. While others planned for college or careers, Jeff seemed completely disengaged. He never talked about the future, and I think now that he never believed that he actually had one. In any event, he seemed completely unmotivated, at times almost inert, and I can only imagine that given the unspeakable visions and desires that had begun to overwhelm him at that time, he must have come to view himself as utterly outside the human community, outside all that was normal and acceptable, outside all that could be admitted to another human being. At least to himself, he was already a prisoner, already one of the condemned.

But the visible manifestations of Jeff's spiritual and emotional descent were slight, at least when compared to the depth of that descent. There was no screaming in the night, no rambling speech, no moments of catatonic blankness. He didn't hear or see things that weren't there. He never exploded suddenly, never so much as raised his voice in either fear or anger. If he had done any of these things, then I might have sensed how deeply he was moving into his madness, and sensing that, I might not only have saved him somehow, but all the others he destroyed, as well.

But rather than demonstrating any blatant show of mental illness, Jeff simply became more quiet and enclosed. Our conversations were reduced to question-and-answer sessions that were really not conversations at all. There was no communication in them, no debate, no sense of information given or received. He never argued, but neither did he ever seem fully to agree with anything. It was as if nothing mattered to him, neither school work nor social relations in or out of school. And yet, even this did not manifest itself as a form of rebellion. Rebellion would have demanded some measure of belief, some expression of his personal convictions. But Jeff was beyond rebellion, and he had no convictions about anything. There were times when I would glimpse him alone in his room, or sitting in front of the television, and it would seem to me that he could not think at all.

I know now what he was thinking of at those times when a blank stare rose into his eyes. And I also know that all those things that were foremost in my son's mind during those years were, in essence, incommunicable, either to me or to anyone else. Even if Jeff had had a friend, he could not have revealed the bizarre and violent impulses that had begun to occupy his mind. How could a teenage boy admit, perhaps even to himself, that the landscape of his developing inner life had become a slaughterhouse? A morgue?

And so, my son went elsewhere with his confusion and distress. He went where millions of others had gone before him, seeking solace or forgetfulness, as he must have been seeking it. He went to the bottle. By the time he finished high school, he was a full-fledged alcoholic. This, however, was completely unknown to me. Preoccupied by the continuing dissolution of my marriage, as well as my duties at work, I remained entirely oblivious to Jeff's drinking. I know now that he took liquor from a neighbor's house, drinking in secret much of the time. I know that he concealed his drinking from me, as any boy would. Moreover, I was often preoccupied with Dave, my other son, and Jeff increasingly slipped by me unawares, a figure who was diminishing before me as a person, even as his body grew.

But as the years passed, it was not only alcoholism into which Jeff sank. By the time he was fifteen, his mind had begun to dissolve completely into a nightmare world. Once that world had taken over completely, it began to dictate every facet of my son's inner life by attaching itself to his developing sexuality, the most powerful force a teenage boy may know. Bizarre notions of death and dismemberment became sexually charged, sexually driven, sexually satisfied.

I can only guess at the inner world into which that process must have hurled my son. I know that as he grew deeper into his adolescence, his face took on an even greater sense of something concealed. In photographs taken near the end of his high school years, his eyes appear more narrow, his gaze more distant, his smile entirely false. During that time, his level of effort sank to the minimum, and at home, he became more withdrawn. His social life, which should have been expanding, narrowed to a circle that was no larger than his mind, an imagined world in which his friends were phantoms, his lovers mere lumps of unmoving flesh.

Jeff hugging his greatest love, Frisky, Barberton, Ohio, 1967

CHAPTER FOUR

Toward the end of 1976, when we were living at Bath Road in Bath, Ohio, a marriage that had been precariously maintained for over sixteen years began its final unraveling. There had been a steady decline since 1970. At that time, Joyce had begun to develop a host of ailments, constipation, insomnia, a nervous condition she described as "fluttering," in which her whole body shook violently and uncontrollably until she finally collapsed into a bedridden exhaustion which would sometimes last for days. For these various illnesses, she took increasingly higher doses of Equanil, along with sleeping pills, laxatives, and Valium.

In order to deal with Joyce's assorted symptoms, her doctor ordered an extensive series of medical tests. None of these tests was able to unearth any specific medical problem, however. Because of that, Joyce's condition was diagnosed as being the result of an "anxiety state," and she was referred to a psychiatrist. She subsequently attended five psychiatric sessions, but they seemed to help her very little.

Finally, in July of 1970, Joyce was admitted to the psychiatric ward of the Akron General Hospital, where she was treated for severe anxiety. She checked herself out after only three days, saying that there was nothing really wrong with her. A few months later, however, she was again hospitalized at Akron General, this time for a month.

Once released, Joyce began to attend group therapy sessions during which she vented her rage against her own father, and actually saw her father's face superimposed over the face of the attending therapist.

However, it was also during that time that Joyce began to make friendships within her group, and once she left it, she maintained those friendships for as long as she could.

She also improved in other ways. She took up making decorative objects of leaded glass, and macramé, and sold a few of her creations at the Hamlet in Bath, Ohio. She spotted a UFO at the intersection of Cleveland and Massillon, chased it at sixty miles an hour, and had the entire story written up in the *Beacon Journal.*

But after a time, her condition started to deteriorate again. She could not lose weight, and a thyroid disorder was diagnosed. The medication did not help her lose weight, however, and Joyce subsequently went to a hypnotist for assistance. At the same time, she began to withdraw from her earlier associations, and our social life collapsed.

Still, even during those last years, there were times when our marriage seemed to rejuvenate somewhat. Joyce's condition would also improve suddenly. During one period of stability, she began to drive. On another occasion, we went on vacation in Puerto Rico. Other events caused me to take hope. She was starting to take classes at Akron University, and leading housewife-growth groups at Portage Path Mental Health Center, the facility to which she'd previously gone for help. However, she was increasingly building a life outside the home, leaving her care and attention to her family to fall by the wayside.

And so, at a far more rapid rate than at any time before, our marriage was moving downward. There were many arguments, and at times, to flee a house that seemed on fire, Jeff, as Dave would tell me later, would walk out into the yard and slap at the trees with branches he'd gathered from the ground.

In my presence, however, as well as when he was in the presence of his mother, Jeff presented an essentially passive demeanor. In the spring of his senior year in high school, for example, we talked quite maturely about his future plans. He would soon be on his own, I told him, and it was time that he began to look toward that approaching independence. The subject turned to college, and he nodded while I made various suggestions about places he should consider. We had fallen into a pattern. My suggestions would be made, routinely accepted, then forgotten. An unbridgeable distance was forming between us, an inability to speak directly to each other. Very often, now, there was the passive mask, the inflexible stare that the world has come to know as the only image of my son.

In August of 1977, Joyce's father died, and when she returned from the funeral she told me that when she'd seen his dead body, she'd felt that our marriage was certainly dead, too. Later, I discovered that she had had an affair.

At last then, it was over. Joyce initiated a divorce. I filed somewhat later, and shortly after that, a custody battle ensued, particularly in regard to David, who was still a child, while Jeff was nearly eighteen years old.

In the end, Joyce was granted custody of David, while I was granted visitation rights on weekends. By agreement, Joyce would sell me the house we'd been living in since the fall of 1967. In the meantime, she would continue to live there, along with Jeff and David, while I took a room not far away at the Ohio Motel.

The divorce proceedings and custody battle had depleted me a great deal. At forty-two, I felt like an old man. Worse, I felt that I had used up a good portion of my life fighting to save a marriage which I should have recognized as doomed almost from the beginning.

I was still in that state of exhaustion and self-recrimination when, about three months before the divorce was finalized, I met a thirty-seven-year-old woman named Shari Jordan. She was working as the personnel manager of a small company on the east side of Cleveland.

The relationship developed quickly. In a sense, I suppose, we were two lonely people. Certainly, I had been completely disoriented by the divorce. Like many men in that condition, particularly those who had thought of family life as a personal achievement, I was left in a fog. Suddenly, I had no one. My wife and children were living in another house, while I had taken up residence at a local motel. My life seemed rather bleak, to say the least. I felt that I was drowning. Needless to say, Shari came to me like a life preserver.

To a great extent, we were completely different, but in a positive, rather than a negative way. Where I was naive in human relations, Shari was astute. Where I had a tendency to avoid conflict, Shari was quick to engage in it, especially when it came down to defending either herself or someone else. She saw through circumstances that remained opaque to me, and her emotional range was much wider than my own. She could feel more than I could feel, but I'm not sure she knew that at the time. Left nearly dumbstruck by my divorce, wandering in the fog of its aftermath, I must have looked terribly vulnerable to her. After all, I had lost almost everything, and in that condition I had to have appeared wounded and adrift, a little boy lost in the storm.

But what Shari didn't know was that I was almost totally analytical. She saw a vulnerable man, one who must have appeared extremely sensitive and accommodating. She could not have seen the other, more disturbing part of me, the part that was often oblivious, that was not very emotional, that had a strange numbness at its core.

Until much later, it was a part that was even invisible to me. But now, when I glimpse Jeff's picture in a book or on the television, I wonder just how close I came to that state of deadness and emotional flatness to which my son at last descended. I look at his face, particularly in photographs taken during his trial, and I see no feeling in him whatsoever, no emotion, only a terrible vacancy in his eyes. I listen to his voice as he describes inconceivable acts. It is a monotone, utterly unaccented and unemotional. I see and hear my son, and I think, "Am I like that?"

My son killed his first human being during the summer of 1978. By then, of course, I was no longer living in the house on Bath Road.

To keep in contact with my sons, particularly with Dave, who was only twelve years old, I often called the house. I would usually talk with Dave, though often with Jeff, as well.

Suddenly, in August, those calls were not answered. I phoned every day for seven days, and there was still no answer. I took to driving by the house, and when, after three days, I had not so much as seen Joyce's car in the driveway, I decided that I had no choice but to check the house.

Shari was with me that day, but she stayed in the car while I got out and headed for the front door.

I knocked at the door, and after a moment, Jeff opened it halfway. He looked somewhat embarrassed, as if he'd been caught off guard.

"Where's your mother?" I asked.

Jeff seemed unprepared to answer my question. "Where's Dave?"

Again, Jeff didn't answer.

Looking into the house, I suddenly noticed that Jeff was not alone.

"Who's in there?" I said as I stepped past Jeff and entered the house.

Joyce and Dave had certainly left, but there were plenty of other people in the house, teenagers of Jeff's acquaintance, all of whom appeared somewhat disoriented and were moving about the house, touching things delicately, as if feeling for their textures.

In short order, I told those strangers to leave, and then began to question Jeff.

"Where are Dave and your mother?" I demanded.

"Gone," Jeff said. "They moved out."

"Moved where?"

"I don't know."

"You mean she's not coming back?" I asked, astonished.

Jeff shrugged.

I continued to question him, but Jeff remained adamant, telling me nothing. He claimed that he did not know where Joyce and Dave had gone, and though I continued to press him, he added nothing beyond his initial, "They moved out."

Shari had walked into the house by then, her first exposure to it, one that was not very pleasant. Almost immediately, as she would say later, she had picked up on its unhappiness. Looking at Jeff, she saw a young man who seemed shell-shocked by the divorce, ashamed and embarrassed by the disarray within his family, a "lost little boy," as she later described him.

During the next few minutes, while I continued to question Jeff, she walked about the house. It was not in a very good state, as she discovered. There was very little food, and the refrigerator was broken. In the family room, she found a round wooden coffee table upon which a pentagram had been drawn in chalk. She called me in to take a look. At the time, I was mystified, but later I learned that Jeff had conducted a séance, that he had been trying to contact the dead.

Not wanting Jeff to remain alone, I moved back into the house right away. Shari came with me. On the day we moved in, Jeff was very polite and helpful. Given the situation, the fact that another woman was moving into the house Jeff had lived in with his mother, Shari found him very kind and helpful. He seemed glad to have me back, and he tried very hard to be pleasant in every way.

Shari and I settled in, hoping to make a home. For a time, things appeared to go quite well. Then, rather suddenly, it changed.

One afternoon, Shari stopped by the house on the way to a doctor's appointment. Passing Jeff's room she noticed the reeking odor of alcohol. She tapped on Jeff's door and he pulled himself off his bed and made his way toward her. Between the smell and Jeff's slurred speech, it was obvious that Jeff was very drunk. "I had a few friends over," he explained, "and we had a few drinks."

Shari called me immediately. "You'd better get home, Lionel," she said, "Jeff's drunk."

Shari had already returned from her appointment when I arrived. She told me that Jeff was still in his room, and I went directly to him. He was still sprawled on the bed, more or less passed out.

His condition both astonished and outraged me. Initially, I was shocked. I had practically no idea that Jeff had ever taken a drink, much less that he had developed a problem with alcohol. I was amazed. "I don't believe this," I said to Shari later, "I just don't believe it."

But the evidence was overwhelming, and so I had no choice but to believe it, and then to deal with it.

I dealt with it by reading Jeff the riot act.

Jeff's reaction was dull and unaccented, a language of shrugs and mumbled responses. He told me that he drank out of boredom, because there was nothing else to do. He volunteered nothing, and after a while, there seemed nothing more to say to him.

During the remaining weeks, while Jeff continued to live in the house on Bath Road, I got no further indication that he was drinking.

However, although we did not know it at the time, he was clearly doing other things. Within two weeks of the drinking episode, Shari discovered that her garnet-and-diamond ring was missing from the jewelry box that she kept in our bedroom. At first, Shari assumed that she might have misplaced the ring, but about two weeks later, a second ring disappeared. This time, there was no question but that it had been stolen.

There had been no forced entry of the house, and no other articles had been taken. Because of that, suspicion fell on a friend of Jeff's, one who had had easy access to the house. Later the police official who had investigated both robberies informed me that Jeff was aware that his friend had stolen Shari's rings.

When confronted with this information, Jeff denied that he had any knowledge of the robberies. He appeared insulted by the accusation, and actually rose to leave the room.

At that moment, Shari, a woman who is over six feet tall in heels and who has a commanding voice, told Jeff in no uncertain terms, that he was to sit back down. For a single, chilling instant, Shari, as she later told me, glimpsed a flash of terrible rage as it passed into Jeff's eyes. In an instant the rage was gone, but in that moment, Shari had seen the other Jeff, the one who looked out from behind the dull, unmoving mask.

But I had seen no such thing. When I told him to sit down, he did as he was told without the slightest show of resistance or emotion. He continued to deny any involvement in the theft, and after a while, the confrontation simply withered away, and Jeff finally trudged to his room and closed the door.

Both figuratively and literally, I made little effort to bring him out again. Over the next month, I worked desperately to find Dave, instead. Since Jeff had continued to tell me that he had no idea where Joyce and Dave were, I had no choice but to look for him in whatever way I could. Because Joyce's family resided in Chippewa Falls, Wisconsin, I concentrated on that area in my search.

For almost a month, I worked at locating my youngest son. I checked telephone information in the hope of finding out that Joyce had gotten a new number, one she'd listed in her own name. I made call after call to my attorney, demanding that she force Joyce's attorney to tell me where she'd taken Dave. I had visitation rights, I told him; she couldn't just take my son away. In the fall, when school finally started, I began calling all the middle schools in the Chippewa Falls area. That strategy paid off, and at last, I located Dave at his new school. It was a tremendous relief to hear his voice.

To the extent that I dealt with Jeff at all during that period, it was to maintain a positive attitude with regard to assuring him that the plans he and I had made amid the throes of the divorce should be carried out. Jeff had, of course, taken the usual SAT test, and I had sent the necessary paperwork and check to Ohio State University for the first quarter. I sensed that he had no enthusiastic interest in it, but, at the same time, I told him, he showed no interest in vocational pursuits, or anything else for that matter. In the end, he eventually went along with the idea of entering college.

In an effort to brighten Jeff's spirits, Shari made a big show of his going to college. By then, he had fully accepted her, so it wasn't hard for her to convince him to accompany her shopping, the two of them picking out his new college clothes. While they shopped, Shari talked about how exciting college was going to be for Jeff, how much he was going to enjoy the new environment, the new people, the fact that it was a whole new experience.

In September of 1978, Shari and I drove Jeff to the Columbus campus of Ohio State University. But despite Shari's efforts, he still went reluctantly, and it was clear that he was going more or less on my orders. He had never exhibited any interest in college or in any of the fields or professions he might pursue there. He had no notion of what his major might be, except some area of business. He packed his bag without excitement and with little thought. Inside the bag, there were none of those articles that one might expect of a young adult. Instead, he had packed a snake skin which he'd gotten at Boy Scout Camp, and two pictures of his dog.

When I returned from the college that night, I felt some relief that my son was gone. Although I still found it difficult to accept his drinking, I found that I had no choice but to do so.

The fact is, I had not been able to find a way either to punish or to correct Jeff. His face was a wall. His eyes were blank. At the time, I thought the alcohol had soaked his brain, drowning what was left of his personality. And yet, there was always a sense of something moving behind his eyes, a thought process that I couldn't reach somehow, as if his mind were locked in a closed chamber, listening only to itself.

I know now what it was listening to. I know the pictures that were flashing through his mind while he slumped motionlessly on the living room sofa, his eyes staring lifelessly out the window.

He was listening to a murder he had already committed several months before. In terror and awesome dread, he was watching it again and again, a horror show that ran ceaselessly behind his moving eyes.

Because the later trial so graphically detailed everything, I even know the individual scenes that must have been playing in my son's mind as he'd sat in the living room, mumbling answers to my questions, nodding spiritlessly as I talked to him about lying and drinking too much. How trivial my complaints must have seemed to him at that time, how small and inconsequential compared to what he had already done.

Now, when I think of him at that point in his life, I see him caught in his own murderous fantasies, trapped in the memory of a murder he had already committed, barely able to connect to any other part of reality. For him, a sudden, uncontrollable act of violence and sexual mutilation had thrust any hope for an ordinary life into a world that was utterly beyond his grasp. How odd and unrealizable all my talk of college and careers must have struck him after that. My ambitions for him, the little strategies I suggested for getting his life on track, must have seemed like constructs from another planet; my system of values, built as it was on notions of work and family, like quaint, but incomprehensible artifacts from a vanished civilization.

The evening tour around university housing, Ames, Iowa, 1964

CHAPTER FIVE

But I knew absolutely nothing about what Jeff had done. Because of that, I was allowed to think of the first quarter during which he was enrolled at Ohio State as a period of renewed hope. During that time, I allowed myself to believe that he had taken the first step in a journey that I hoped would be successful. It was a journey I had made, from a public school senior to a doctorate in chemistry, and I saw no reason why Jeff shouldn't make it, too.

At first, things seemed to go rather well with Jeff. On a later visit, he proudly displayed his room, which was very neat and orderly. Still later, he walked Shari and me around the campus. He seemed proud to be at college. He actually appeared happy.

But it was an illusion of progress that I could not maintain for long.

Jeff's grades came in the mail at the end of the first quarter. They arrived only a few days before Jeff did, and they were a disaster. With a cumulative grade point of only .45, he had earned two hours of college credit after a full quarter in Columbus. He had failed

Introduction to Anthropology. He had not completed Greco-Roman History. His performance in Administrative Science had been no more than mediocre, and he had dropped other courses after only a few weeks. His highest grade had been a B − in Riflery. He had distinguished himself in nothing.

When Shari and I drove down to pick him up and bring him back home, he seemed, like always, embarrassed and ashamed. He offered a few hastily constructed excuses, none of them very convincing. Concerning his failure at college, Jeff explained that he had simply found it difficult to get up for his morning classes. As for his other classes, they had slipped beyond his control somehow. He did not know why or how.

One thing was clear, as I told him later: he would not be returning to the University. When I told him that I had no intention of returning him to college, he looked relieved, as if a burden had been lifted from his shoulders. It could hardly have been more clear that my decision held no consequences for him. Knowing what he already knew about himself, of course, how could he have regarded college with any seriousness at all?

A few days later, Shari and I once again drove to Columbus, this time to pick up Jeff's things. His room was a quad, and Jeff's part of it was extremely neat, the bed made, his closet well ordered. The only note of alarm was a row of beer and wine bottles which he had lined up along the top of his closet.

His roommates were lounging casually in the room, and as we began to gather Jeff's things, I spoke with them. What emerged from that brief conversation was a portrait of my son that was the most alarming anyone had yet given me. Jeff, they said, most definitely had a drinking problem. He drank every day. Often, he would drink himself into a stupor, finally passing out late in the evening. In the mornings, unable to rise, he would remain sprawled on his bed until the middle of the afternoon. He had made no effort to control his drinking. In fact, the only efforts he had made at all were those designed to make sure that he had a full supply of liquor. As we later discovered, that included selling his own blood plasma at a local blood bank, a practice he had engaged in so often that the blood center had finally marked his name, preventing him from making visits too frequently.

Once we returned home, I told Jeff that it was time for him to do something. College was out. His choices were down to only two. He either had to get a job, or he had to join one of the armed services.

One morning not long after that, I dropped Jeff at Summit Mall, from which he could make his way either to the State Employment Service or, perhaps, to any other place that might have an opening.

By then, of course, I had come to accept the fact

that larger and less ordinary opportunities no longer existed for Jeff. He had closed one door after another. Now the doors were few, but it still seemed possible that he might find at least one still open to him, one that would allow him to live a life that made sense to him, that afforded him some measure of dignity, security, perhaps even a degree of pleasure and self-esteem.

For the next few days, I picked Jeff up in the late afternoon at Summit Mall. Sometimes he seemed quite normal, but at other times it was obvious that he had been drinking during the day. His eyes would glisten drunkenly, and he was often unsteady on his feet. He would answer my questions in mumbled slurs. On one occasion, he arrived at my car dead drunk. I felt that I simply could not return him to my house in that state. Shari had been through enough. We had been married for only a short time by then, and Jeff had made those early months a considerable burden. I realized that it was time to say no to him.

And so, I said no. I told him that I would not take him home drunk, that I had had enough. I told him that he had to stay at the mall until he was sober. Once he had sobered up, he could call me, and I would come and get him. Then I left him there, standing in the mall parking lot, drove home, and waited for his call.

But it was a call that never came. At ten that same

night, I drove back to the mall. All the stores were closed, and there was no sign of Jeff. I went back home and called the police. It had taken only that one call to locate my son. He had been picked up several hours before, booked on a charge of drunk and disorderly conduct, and taken to jail.

I went directly to police headquarters and bailed Jeff out. A few minutes later, we were in my car and I was taking him home. Jeff sat quietly, his head hung low. At home, he apologized to me and to Shari, then once again entered the solitude of his bedroom.

Morning brought an ultimatum. Jeff by then had refused counseling. He had refused to get a job. The last doors were closing. Only one was left. I told my son point-blank that it was time to get his life together. He was not functioning in the world around him, it seemed to me, and so he needed a separate, less open world. It was time for him to go through the last door still open to him.

Jeff joined the United States Army in January of 1979. I drove him to the recruiting office myself. I had already talked to a recruiting sergeant and set up the interview. On the way to the office, Jeff seemed resigned, though not exactly sad. Once at the office, he went through the necessary forms as if on automatic pilot.

By the end of January, Jeff was gone. We said good-bye at the recruiting office. More than anything, he seemed afraid. He knew that he now faced a very different life, more rigorous, more demanding. It would be a way of life that would not in the least tolerate either the one addiction I already knew about, alcoholism, or the other, darker and far more nightmarish one, which Jeff had managed to keep locked entirely within himself.

I did not see Jeff for six months. When I did see him again, the transformation was difficult to believe. The Jeff I picked up at the bus station in downtown Akron was astonishingly different from the frightened boy I'd seen at the recruiting station.

This new, completely refurbished Jeff was a handsome, broad-shouldered young man who smiled brightly when he stepped off the bus. His hair was close-cropped, his clothes neat and orderly. More important, perhaps, there was not so much as a hint of liquor on his breath.

He stayed with Shari and me for no more than a couple of weeks. For the first time in his life, he seemed bent on being of service. He helped me chop and stack wood. He raked leaves and picked up fallen branches. When we weren't working, we played tennis, or cooked outside. On the grill, he would cook hamburgers and steaks. Through it all, he wore a bright, self-confident smile.

Not far away, at the top of a hill, the dismembered body of Jeff's first victim lay in a storm drain, still unmoved and undiscovered, but the brutal young man who had carried out his murder could not have been glimpsed in the trim and cheerful young man who sat across from me at dinner, talking proudly of his time in the army.

For the entire two weeks that Jeff remained at home with us, I saw only the positive changes that had come over him: the way he talked more freely, the way his eyes looked at me with an unexpected openness. I could remember the morose figure who slouched in my living room and trudged sullenly toward his room, and I allowed myself to think that this other Jeff had been run to ground by the rigors of basic training.

The two weeks of Jeff's visit ended quickly. It had passed in an atmosphere that was cheerful and relaxed. On Jeff's last day, I drove him to the bus that would take him to Cleveland. After that, he would be sent to Germany. This time, Jeff sat in the passenger seat, his head erect, his eyes firmly set. All the fear and dread I'd seen at our earlier parting had disappeared. When we arrived, he hugged me and stepped onto the bus. As it pulled away, he faced the window and waved good-bye.

*   *   *

During the next two years, we received few letters, despite the fact that Shari wrote often, sending pictures of the house, the garden, all that was going on at home. But Jeff had never been much of a writer, and so the lack of correspondence was not something that surprised me. However, he did call once or twice.

During those calls, he seemed to be enjoying his tour, and even when he didn't, when the conversation was short and clipped, I allowed myself to believe that he was only tired, that somewhere in Germany the "new" Jeff was alive and well and still at the task of building a decent future for himself. When I thought of him, I saw him in uniform, and I thought of that uniform and all that it represented as his salvation. The army had provided a structure for his profoundly unstructured life, and I hoped, perhaps even allowed myself to believe, that in that structure Jeff had actually found a home.

Then, suddenly, three months before his military service was up, Jeff's trunk arrived on my doorstep. Inside, I found his army fatigues, his jacket and trousers, everything, it seemed, that he could possibly have possessed at the time he had been mustered out of the army. There was no note, no letter, nothing that might give me the slightest idea as to where Jeff was.

A few days later, Jeff's military discharge papers arrived in the mail. They stated that Jeff had been given an honorable discharge, though a code number indicated that the discharge had been given for a particular reason. In Jeff's case, that reason, as we later found out, was alcoholism.

But in all those papers, there was still no indication as to where Jeff had gone. He had been mustered out in North Carolina, but I had no idea where he might have gone after that. It was another month before I knew.

Then one Saturday morning, the phone rang. It was Jeff. He said that he was calling from Miami, Florida. He seemed quite happy. He was, he told me, working at a sandwich and pizza place called the Sunshine Sub Shop. He added few details, and I did not ask for more. He was on his own now, far away, beyond my ability to get to him quickly if he found himself in trouble. I allowed myself to think of the distance in a positive light, as if, merely by staying away, Jeff was growing into adulthood. Over the next few weeks, he called occasionally, his voice clipped, the conversations short, which was not unusual. In one conversation, he told me that he was now living with a woman, an illegal alien, who had offered him money to marry her, something we advised him not to do.

The final phone call had to do with money. Jeff had run out of it again, completely out, and without any means of getting more. He asked Shari to send him some money right away, but she refused. She told him that the only "money" she would send him was a plane ticket to Cleveland. If he wanted to come home, she would bring him back. She told him that she wouldn't send him the money for the ticket, but that she would have a ticket waiting for him at the airport.

Jeff agreed to come home. He didn't protest. He seemed resigned, as if, once again, he was having to give up an independence he had been unable to maintain.

I picked him up at the Cleveland airport a few days later, expecting a scruffy, downtrodden young man, crestfallen and humiliated. As he came off the plane, however, he was smiling brightly, and from a distance, he looked amazingly cheerful. But as he came closer, I realized that he was drunk, and that it was this that had made him appear cheerful.

"Sorry, Dad," Jeff said as he stepped up to me. "I guess I had a few too many on the plane."

Once he'd come closer to me, I saw that Jeff was filthy and disheveled. He'd grown a moustache which he hadn't cleaned or tended and was now scraggly and unkempt. His clothes were unwashed and covered with stains. He stank of whiskey, and a cigarette dangled from the corner of his mouth.

But within days, he'd brightened again. Once at home, he simply couldn't be helpful enough. He chopped wood, helped take down a tree, and gathered fallen branches. It was as if the army had given him a work ethic, or at least had helped him to gain the will to do things, even when he didn't want to do them.

One afternoon, with winter coming on, we decided to wrap the water pipes with insulation. He helped in the attic, but when it came to wrapping the pipes down in the crawl space, he insisted on doing that himself. "No, don't go down there, Dad," he said emphatically. "Let me do that."

And so, it was Jeff who went into the crawl space where he had once stored the body of his first victim. I could see him on his back, wrapping insulation around the lines of copper pipes, then tying it in place with a thick, braided twine. When he came out again, he dusted himself off, cheerful and enthusiastic, ready for the next household task.

But this rebirth lasted for only a few days. Soon Jeff began to look for a job. I would either drop him off at Summit Mall or leave him the car so that he could look for work. Inevitably, when he was alone, he began to drink.

Only two weeks after returning home, Jeff was arrested at the local Ramada Inn. He'd been asked to leave the lounge because he'd been drinking straight out of a vodka bottle. He had refused to do that, and so he'd been taken to the lobby. Even then, however, he hadn't gone away. Instead, he'd hung around the front door, still drinking from the bottle. The police had finally been called, and at their arrival, Jeff had suddenly turned violent. It had taken three officers to restrain him. Arrested, and later charged with drunk and disorderly conduct, Jeff had been taken to the Akron Correctional Facility.

Jeff's brief incarceration did no good, and after the episode at the Ramada Inn, the drinking never really stopped, at least not while he lived with Shari and me. At times, he would lose his glasses or wallet while drunk. Several times, he even lost track of the car. As the weeks passed, the calls continued. They might come from Jeff, from a bartender, or from the police, but always the call was to tell me that Jeff was drunk, that he couldn't drive, that I had to come and get him.

By the winter of 1981, Shari and I had decided that Jeff's life had begun to unravel, that he had to get control of himself, and that he could not do that while living at home. A week before, I had taken him to the Ohio Motel to dry out overnight. I had told him that he needed to use that time alone to rethink his life, somehow to get a grip on it.

The question, then, was what to do with Jeff. Both Shari and I were at our wits' end. Since the Bath Road house was in the country, we didn't feel that we could leave Jeff alone all day, with little or nothing to do. Under such conditions, we knew he would drink. Neither could we trust him with the car, even to use it for job interviews, since he had also gotten drunk on such occasions.

After a lot of discussion, Shari and I finally suggested that Jeff visit his grandmother in West Allis, Wisconsin, a suburb of Milwaukee. He had always seemed to love my mother, and there was certainly no question but that she loved him.

And so, once again, I found myself at the bus station with my son. His demeanor was the one I had come to expect at such moments: resigned, somewhat contrite, generally passive and without emotion, the sense, perhaps, that once again he was being rejected.

As I said good-bye to him, I fully expected him to return after a brief visit. Certainly I did not sense that anything dangerous lurked behind his nearly blank, unmoving face. I hugged him, as I always had, as any father might, and wished him well.

On the way home, I thought over the situation, trying to come to terms with it as best I could. I had a wayward son, as other fathers had, and I hoped that somewhere in the covering darkness that stretched between Bath, Ohio, and West Allis, Wisconsin, some light might dawn on him, a tiny point that might guide him safely home.

*Jeff and Lee having sherbet and ginger ale treats,
Halloween, Barberton, Ohio, 1967*

CHAPTER SIX

Approximately three months later, Shari and I drove up to West Allis to visit Jeff at my mother's house. By that time, Jeff had decided that he would not return to Ohio. He had found life at my mother's house very congenial. She mothered him shamelessly, cooked for him, and washed his clothes. It was little wonder that I found Jeff far happier than at any time since he'd come home from the army.

For all of us, this period—which was to cover a full six years—was one of great hope. During all of that time, my son appeared to be adjusting quite well. He mowed my mother's lawn, worked in her garden, and helped her with her shopping and the house cleaning. He went to church with her, as well, and my mother reported that a young woman in the congregation had developed an interest in Jeff, one which I encouraged him to pursue.

"You should call her up, Jeff," I told him.

"Yeah, I should," he replied, "but I just haven't gotten around to it."

It was similarly encouraging to me that Jeff had

gotten a job as a phlebotomist at the Milwaukee Blood Plasma Center, and had begun attending counseling sessions at Alcoholics Anonymous. All of these developments were evidence, it seemed to me, of a life that appeared to be on a better course.

During all this time, I continued to live in the hope that the Jeff who lived in West Allis, held down a job, and treated my mother with kindness was the real Jeff, essentially good, a young man searching for himself, as I supposed many others were searching. I knew that I did not have the answer to my son, that I did not possess any particular insight into his character, and that, for these insights, I depended more and more on Shari.

I was not the only one who had come to depend upon her, however. At the end of that promising six years, when Jeff began to abandon his more positive direction, my mother increasingly came to Shari with disturbing reports concerning his behavior. She was reluctant to come to me, she said, because she didn't want to burden me, or perhaps she didn't want to interfere with what she saw as my own naïveté in regard to Jeff. Thus, over a period of many months, my mother reported to Shari, rather than to me, talking to her on the telephone, relating those aspects of Jeff's life which could not be reconciled with my continuing hope that he had straightened out.

It was through Shari, then, that I learned that the

hopeful period of Jeff's reformation was slowly coming to an end, that he was drifting downward again.

During one such conversation, my mother told Shari that she had found a full-size department store manikin in Jeff's closet. It was a male figure, fully dressed in sports shirt and shorts. My mother could not imagine how Jeff had gotten such a thing. Had he ordered it? Stolen it? In either case, why? She could not imagine to what purpose Jeff might put so curious an object. Very clearly, she expected someone to get to the bottom of it.

This was the strangest tale anyone had ever related about Jeff, and not long after Shari had told me about it, I called him up. I told him that I knew about the manikin, and that I wanted to know where it had come from, and why it had ended up in his closet.

Jeff's reaction was completely calm and unemotional. He said that he'd taken it from a store only to demonstrate that he could do it. He said he'd rather liked the clothes that were on the manikin, but that the taking of the manikin, itself, had been nothing more than a prank, the response to a challenge he'd offered himself, a bit of derring-do.

Typically, I clicked into the details.

"Well, how'd you do it, Jeff?" I asked.

In response, Jeff told me that he'd taken the torso apart at the middle, and placed each half in a separate shopping bag. After that, he'd simply strolled out of the store. I reminded him that this was a theft, and demanded that he return everything to the store. Jeff told me that he'd already thrown both the manikin and its clothing away, and that the issue, as far as he was concerned, was closed. As to any analysis of his action, there was none. He had acted on an impulse which was natural to him. He'd wanted something, so he'd taken it. It was as simple as that.

But to Shari, it was not so simple. To her, the manikin suggested that something was deeply wrong with Jeff. She did not know what it was, but only that no young man of his age should have a male manikin in his closet.

"There's something wrong with this story," she told me. "I don't know what it is, but there's something wrong."

I decided to offer Jeff a plan, a way of moving forward in his life. We met at the house in West Allis, the two of us seated in the living room, staring directly at each other. Jeff sat very erect in a chair by the window and listened as I ticked off the possibilities: a business of his own, such as Amway or some other independent sales position; technical or vocational school, some form of highly specific training; perhaps even gardening, which he had seemed to enjoy, at least so far as I had observed him when he worked in the yard around my house. Last, I suggested that he go to a job-counseling facility, either private or public—

some place that might give him options which, so far, he himself had not thought about.

Through it all, Jeff nodded appreciatively, repeating, in a kind of numb chant, "Sounds reasonable, sounds reasonable, could be a possibility."

This response, though typical of Jeff, nonetheless gave me some encouragement, so I drove Jeff down to the Milwaukee Area Technical College. I walked him through the entire enrollment procedure. We met with one of the school counselors, selected two courses, then went through the final steps involved in Jeff's matriculation. I paid the bill for his tuition, and drove him back to my mother's house.

Later, Shari and I drove back to Ohio. On the way, I allowed myself a bit of optimism as to Jeff's future, and did as much as possible to deny the darker elements of his character. Shari was less hopeful. She believed that Jeff had only gone along with something I wanted, and even then, very reluctantly.

A few weeks later, Shari's pessimism was confirmed. I called my mother to see how Jeff was doing. By then, I had at least learned that I could not rely on my son's version of anything. My mother told me that as far as she knew, Jeff had not gone to school at all. I immediately called the school and found out that my mother was right. Jeff had not attended a single class.

When I later talked to Jeff, I asked him why he had not bothered to attend classes. He told me that he'd been unable to go to classes because he'd gotten a job with a temporary agency. This, he thought, was a better step for him.

That he had not bothered to let me know of that choice, did not occur to him. It meant nothing to him that he had wasted both my money and my time.

And yet, true to the contradictory nature of Jeff's character, he had actually gotten a job at a temporary agency. In that regard, he had told the truth, something that, when I learned of it, actually surprised me. He had become that most artful of all deceivers, one who mixes falsehood with just a pinch of truth.

Still, his lies seemed relatively harmless. His life, for all its disorder and lack of purpose, still seemed essentially harmless. For all Jeff had done, at least as far as I knew of what he had done, he had harmed no one but himself. I had no reason to believe that he would ever do otherwise.

Then my mother telephoned to tell me that she had found a gun underneath Jeff's bed, and that she had no idea where it had come from or what he intended to use it for.

Once again, I called Jeff. I told him that his grandmother had discovered the gun he kept under his bed, and that it had frightened her. Jeff tried to minimize her fears. He said that the gun was only a target pistol, and that he'd bought it to use on a shooting range not far away. It had no other use, he said, there was nothing to be worried about. I told him that it was still something that frightened his grandmother, and that he should keep it in a box until I saw him again.

Shari and I drove to Milwaukee a week later. Jeff showed me the gun. It was not a target pistol. Far from it. It was a Colt Lawman .357 Magnum with a two-and-a-half-inch barrel, and I told him that such weapons were not the type that one found at a shooting range. Jeff explained that it didn't matter that it was not actually a target pistol, because the shooting range accepted any kind of gun, and that the targets were very close. Because of that, he went on, he had not needed an official, long-barreled target pistol, and so he had bought the .357 Magnum instead. Despite Jeff's explanation, I took the gun from him, asked a friend to sell it, and later gave the proceeds of the sale to Jeff.

A short time later, there was another report from West Allis. My mother called to say that Jeff was often away from home for long periods, sometimes whole weekends. His excuse was that he liked to roam a nearby mall, or that he had gone to Chicago to hang out for a while.

More ominous from my mother's point of view was another incident. One morning, she had been on her way down the stairs when Jeff had abruptly called for her to stop.

"I'm not dressed," he'd told her, and asked my mother to go back up the stairs.

Somewhat later, however, she had seen Jeff again. This time with a man who appeared to be drunk, and whom Jeff was obviously trying to get to the nearest bus stop. The man had staggered as he walked, and had even fallen down a few times before Jeff had finally managed to get to the bus.

To my subsequent questions, Jeff had ready answers. The man was someone he had met casually and, just as casually, had decided to bring home for a while. It had been late at night, and not wanting to disturb his grandmother, Jeff had decided to take the man down into the basement of the house to sleep in an old tilt-back chair. In addition, he said, they had drunk too much already, and he didn't want the man throwing up in his grandmother's house. Once in the basement, Jeff and his guest had drunk a bit more, and when Jeff thought the other man was sufficiently sober, he'd simply taken him to the bus stop and put him on a bus.

Like the manikin, the man was gone, and as far as Jeff was concerned, the case was closed.

But for every odd thing that Jeff explained away, something else arose to take its place.

One Sunday morning, my mother drove into her garage at West Allis and was suddenly overwhelmed by a horrible odor. She could not imagine what it was, and when she asked Jeff about it, he told her that the odors came from the cat box.

But the odor my mother detected did not smell like a cat box and so, still sheltering me from any disturbing news about my son, she called Shari, who, of course, later spoke to me.

I called Jeff immediately, and he explained that he often had time on his hands, and that he liked to experiment with bleaches and muriatic acid on old chicken parts which he bought from a local grocery store. He told me that he simply wanted to see what the chemicals would do to the chicken parts.

Several months later, again after driving into the garage following Sunday services, my mother smelled strange odors. Again, she confronted Jeff, who told her that he'd cleaned the garage floor and that the residual smells were from the chemical cleaners he'd used in the process.

But the odors my mother had detected did not smell like any cleaner she had ever used. She again called us to express her concern with what Jeff was doing.

I promptly made arrangements to fly to West Allis so that I could investigate the odors personally. After checking the garage, I again confronted Jeff, pressing him for answers, until he finally admitted the "truth." While out walking, he told me, he'd seen a dead raccoon in a gutter several streets away. He'd gathered its remains in a garbage bag and brought them home. As to why he'd brought them home, Jeff answered that he'd wanted to experiment on the carcass, using bleach and various chemicals. "I know it sounds stupid," he told me, "but I just wanted to see what the chemicals would do."

I continued to question him, but Jeff stuck to his story. He repeated again and again that it had been a "dumb idea," but that the raccoon and chemical mixes were gone now, and that the issue, as in the case of the manikin, was therefore closed.

But it was not closed. I continued to press him.

"But why would you be adding chemicals to these things?" I asked.

"Just to experiment."

"But what kind of experiment, Jeff?"

"Just an experiment. To see what would happen."

"But what would be the point of that?"

Then there was the familiar shrug. "I know it's stupid, Dad, but I just like to experiment."

But it was so stupid, so utterly pointless and childish an experiment that I decided to look into it a bit further. I searched through the garage, then went down into the basement. I found nothing in the garage, other than a thick, black liquid in the area where my mother kept her large metal garbage cans, and which I supposed to be nothing more sinister than the drippings from the meat and vegetable matter which she regularly deposited in the cans. In the basement, I found only what I might have expected—things in storage, an old movie projector, old lamps, Christmas decorations, some firewood, along with my mother's washer and dryer.

The next day, I returned to Ohio. On the way, I allowed myself to believe Jeff, to accept all his answers regardless of how implausible they might seem. I allowed myself to believe that my son had not intended to do anything illegal with the pistol and that the smells my mother had detected in the basement and the garage had come from the desiccated remains of a dead raccoon.

More than anything, I allowed myself to believe that there was a line in Jeff, a line he wouldn't cross. It was the line that divided the harm he did to himself from the harm he might do to someone else. In the most general sense, I knew that Jeff had failed to make a life for himself. I knew that he had done poorly in school, and had been unsuccessful in the army. I knew that he had been unable to find anything that seemed to interest him, or to which he could attach himself. I knew that he had not been able to maintain a lasting relationship with anyone outside his immediate family.

I also had to admit that there was a darker side to Jeff, though I didn't allow myself to consider where this darker side might lead.

And so, my life had become an exercise in

avoidance and denial. I had grasped at every hope, evaded every unpleasant truth. In the months that followed, my conversations with Jeff continued on the same, anesthetized plane they'd been on from the time he was a teenage boy. We spoke, but we did not converse. I made suggestions. He accepted them. He gave excuses. I accepted them. It was as if we had agreed to speak only in half sentences, communicating only what it was safe to communicate, and never moving to penetrate the wall that had come to exist between us.

Now, when I think of those final days, I see myself in a kind of mental crouch, half expecting some sudden blow, but hoping against hope that it would never hit. I had come to accept the wall that separated me from my son. I had even come to think of it not so much as a wall, but as a shield which both of us needed if we were to communicate at all. It was as if we had agreed to speak only of the most banal things, because each of us knew that there were other things which, if honestly confronted, would tear us both apart. We had tacitly agreed to severely limit the subjects about which we could talk. We would discuss only the most trivial things in life, and let all the more profound and troubling ones drop from our conversations. We would live in a world of shallow exchanges, and let everything else remain unsaid. This dreadful silence we called peace.

Jeff, fresh from basic training, with Dave and Lionel, Bath, Ohio, 1979

CHAPTER SEVEN

B y the fall of 1988, there were far, far more things that I did *not* know about my son than I did know about him. Certainly, I didn't know that he had already killed four human beings, two of them in the basement of my mother's house.

But in addition to such horrible, nearly incomprehensible knowledge, I didn't know that he had been twice arrested for indecent exposure, first in 1982, then in 1986. I didn't know that in 1985, while sitting in the West Allis Library, a man had passed him a note, telling him that if he wanted "a blow job," he should come to the second-floor men's room, and that it was this note, as Jeff would later say, that had sent him spiraling downward at an ever-increasing speed, first to the bathhouses, where he had used drugs to knock out various guests so that he could "lay" with their motionless bodies, and then, still later, into that even deeper and more unfathomable descent.

*　　*　　*

On September 26, 1988, Jeff moved out of his grandmother's house in West Allis. Three years before, he had taken a job at the Ambrosia Chocolate Factory in Milwaukee, and had told me that he wanted to live closer to his work. In addition, he said he wanted to live on his own.

Of course, he had long ago reached the age at which he had that right, so I made no attempt to persuade him to stay with his grandmother. She was old and frail, and Jeff's frequent absences from the house had strained their relationship. In addition, by that time, she had found various articles of occult worship in Jeff's room, and they had terrified her. She was a life-long Presbyterian, and the fact that her own grandson had set up a kind of Satanic altar in her house, complete with griffins and bizarre black lights, was horrifying.

When confronted with these things, Jeff had offered his usual answers. Statues of griffins and a copy of *The Satanic Bible* were only evidence of the "dabbling" with religion he'd gotten into. They meant nothing. He was not a Satanist, just a person who was curious about the unknown.

These were the kind of dismissive answers so typical of Jeff; I think that perhaps he had simply grown tired of giving any answer at all. He wanted to live alone so that he would never again have to answer to anyone.

He left my mother's house, moved his belongings into an apartment house, and prepared to make it on his own. The structures that had shielded, and to some extent controlled, him, had suddenly disappeared. For the first time since Joyce had left him alone in the house at the age of eighteen, Jeff was living by himself.

On the very first day of this new life, Jeff approached a thirteen-year-old Laotian boy named Somsack Sinthasomphone, and took him to his new place, Apartment 204 on North Twenty-fourth Street in Milwaukee. He offered him fifty dollars to pose in the nude while he took photographs. Then he drugged him with a mixture of coffee, Baileys Irish Cream, and benzodiazepine. A few minutes later, while taking pictures, and after having asked Sinthasomphone if he could lie next to him and listen to his stomach, Jeff fondled the boy's penis.

Still under the influence of the drug Jeff had used to disable and sexually molest him, Sinthasomphone had finally fled the apartment and returned to his own home. His family had then rushed him to the hospital, where the overdose was detected.

The police were then summoned, and while Sinthasomphone labored to recover, they asked him where he'd gotten the drug. Once on his feet again, the boy took police officers to Jeff's apartment. Jeff was not at home when they arrived, but detectives soon determined that he worked as a mixer at nearby Ambrosia Chocolate. It was there that they arrested him.

After receiving the phone call that informed me of these things, I realized for the first time that Jeff had, in fact, crossed that line which divides willful self-destruction from the equally willful destruction of another. Somsack Sinthasomphone had been an innocent victim, by law a child, and my son had purposely lured him to his new apartment, drugged, and then sexually abused him.

Upon hearing this news, I was outraged, even though by then, I had ceased to be surprised by anything Jeff might do. In any event, I only remember going through the necessary motions in order to ensure that Jeff would get whatever he needed in his current situation. I found an attorney to defend Jeff, and made the necessary arrangements for my mother to make his two-thousand-dollar bail.

A few days later, Jeff was released. Once again, he looked as he had so often on such occasions—embarrassed, ashamed, deeply depressed.

"I'll never do anything like that again, Dad," he assured me.

But with this assurance came another lie.

"I didn't know he was a kid," Jeff said.

In fact, the boy had told Jeff his age almost immediately after meeting him.

Jeff admitted taking pictures of Sinthasomphone,

but he said he had only brushed up against the boy's penis while unzipping his pants. He had not touched it on purpose. That had been an inadvertent act, merely a motion he'd made while taking photographs. He had meant no harm. He was, as always, sorry for the trouble he had caused.

Beyond an embarrassed "Sorry, Dad," I got very little more from Jeff during the time we spent together before his sentencing. He moved into my mother's house in West Allis again, while I returned to Ohio. I visited him a few times after that, and he would sometimes call, but any deeper sense of togetherness seemed beyond us now. We never once talked about what he had done. He never mentioned the young boy he'd molested. It was as if once an act was committed, all future reference to it was immediately dismissed. I felt as though I could not question him, and he would not volunteer anything. We maintained the wall, both of us guarding it, I think now, with an equal determination. The terrified little boy I'd once rescued from the sucking earth was now unquestionably beyond my reach.

When Jeff was released on bail, the conditions of his release required that he return to my mother's house.

Eight months passed between the time of Jeff's release and the date of his sentencing. During all of that time, he lived with my mother.

On the day before Jeff was scheduled to be sentenced for child molestation, I drove to my mother's house in West Allis in order to accompany Jeff to his court appearance.

He had packed most of his clothes, but as I went through his room, I found a small wooden box with a metal rim. It was about one foot square, and its lid was tightly sealed and locked.

"What's in here?" I asked.

"Nothing."

"Open it up, Jeff."

He didn't move. I could see that he was agitated, but carefully controlling it. His nervousness confirmed what was then my suspicion. I had previously found a few pornographic magazines, and I suspected that he had stored others in the locked wooden box. Since I didn't want my mother to happen upon such things, I demanded that he open it.

"But why, Dad?," Jeff asked. "There's nothing in it."

"Open it."

Jeff suddenly grew very alarmed. "Can't I have just one foot of space to myself. Do you have to look through everything?"

"What's in the box, Jeff?"

"Just one square foot?" Jeff asked. He looked hurt. "Just one?"

I remained adamant.

"I want to know what's in the box, Jeff," I said firmly.

Jeff did not move to open it.

I turned and started for the basement to get a tool with which I could open the box myself.

Jeff leaped in front of me. He whipped out a birthday check I had written only the day before and ripped it up. "I don't want this if you can't give me one foot of privacy."

I stared at him silently, and Jeff very quickly calmed himself.

"You're right, Dad," he said quietly. "It's magazines, that kind of thing. But just leave it for now, OK? It might upset Grandma. I'll open it for you in the morning, I promise." He walked back into the kitchen and tucked the box beneath his arm. "I'll open it in the morning," he said, as he disappeared into the basement.

The next morning, Jeff returned with the box. He took a key from his pocket and opened it. "See?" he said.

I glanced down in to a stack of pornographic magazines.

"Get rid of that stuff before your grandmother sees it," I told him.

"OK, Dad," Jeff said obediently, then he closed the box and returned to the basement.

Later that same morning, May 23, 1989, Judge William D. Gardner sentenced Jeff to five years probation and required him to serve one year in a work-release program centered at the Milwaukee County House of Correction in downtown Milwaukee.

Before sentencing, Jeff spoke directly to the judge. He was very contrite. He told the judge that he understood the nature of his crime and that he was ashamed of having committed it. He asked the judge to be lenient. He said he hoped that he would be given another chance.

As I listened to him, I found that, against all odds, I still believed that it was possible for Jeff to be saved. By that time I had discovered that prior to this last arrest, Jeff had been arrested for exposing himself to teenage boys at the state fairground. Much later still, I learned that while on bail, he had killed yet another human being, and that the box he'd refused to open had contained a human head. And yet, since I knew nothing of these things, I continued to hope that Jeff, perhaps through the intervention of a jail sentence, would finally be able to get control of his life.

And so, on the day Jeff was sentenced, I could still see him as the little boy who'd laughed raucously and played in the yard with his dog, the one I'd taken fishing and skating and to the movies, the little boy I'd hugged a thousand times.

Watching him as he faced the judge that day, it was hard to believe that this same son would never be more than he seemed to be—a liar, an alcoholic, a thief, an exhibitionist, a molester of children. I could not imagine how he had become such a ruined soul, and, incredible as it now seems to me, I let myself believe that even all these grotesque and repulsive behaviors could be thought of as a stage through which he would one day pass.

In the eyes of parents, I think, children always seem just a blink away from redemption. No matter to what depth we watch them sink, we believe they need only grasp the lifeline, and we can still pull them safely to shore. For many years, I had been just that naive, a father who'd grasped at every straw, believed every lie, extended one hand after another, and through it all, continued to believe that there was something salvageable in the wreckage of his son.

As failure had mounted upon failure, and I had seen Jeff sink deeper and deeper, I had nonetheless continued to provide my share of the spiritual, intellectual, and financial support by which he could still reach a decent life.

But as I watched Jeff speak to the judge, I felt a sudden sense of my own helplessness. Suddenly, and for the first time, I no longer believed that *my* efforts and resources alone would be enough to save my son.

I saw a young man in whom something essential was missing. I saw a young man who fundamentally lacked that element of will which allows a human being to take hold of and direct his own life. From that time forward, and even as I watched Jeff being led away to serve his year at the House of Correction, I knew that if he were ever to be "corrected," it would only be through the intercession of some power other than my own. It might be God, I thought. Or it might be the State. It might be some counseling program. Or it might simply be another person who, against all odds, could teach him how to live a better life. Whatever force it was, it would have to come from outside Jeff, and it would not be me.

From then on, I began to look for that external solution. I no longer believed that my own prodding could help my son. I no longer believed that I could support the collective weight of his descent. Because of that, I knew that there would be no more sitting down at the table to plan his future, no more helpful and well-meaning suggestions about education or career, no more pretending that he was just a wayward youth. My son had passed beyond the reach of ordinary care.

While Jeff remained at the House of Correction, I tried to secure the kind of help I thought he needed. I wrote numerous letters to Gerald Boyle, Jeff's attorney. Each letter was more emphatic than the last, and as the months passed, and Jeff's release grew nearer, I became more and more determined to find some sort of independent help for my son.

But in some things, I was blind, as well. I continued to see Jeff's problems as primarily connected to his alcoholism. I allowed myself to believe that if that addiction could be addressed, then his other behaviors would correct themselves. I did not want to confront the fact that Jeff was lost to more than alcoholism. As long as I could see him simply as a victim of alcoholism, I could continue to believe that there might still be a future for him somewhere, a life that might be something more than the long downward spiral it had been thus far.

I wrote letter after letter to Jeff's lawyer, all of them pleading that Jeff be placed in some kind of highly structured treatment program. I was convinced that if Jeff left prison without being rid of his alcoholism, then he would continue to commit acts of sexual assault and molestation. In my view, it was my son's dependence on alcohol that weakened his will to resist these other, even more dangerous and destructive impulses.

Lost in that illusion, I made every effort to get Jeff placed in an effective alcohol treatment program. I told Jeff's attorney that I did not think he should be allowed an early release from prison, in view of the fact that he had received no alcohol treatment while in prison. Mr. Boyle replied that the matter of treatment should be taken up with Jeff's probation officer, and that as Jeff's lawyer, it was his duty to seek early release if that was what Jeff wanted, which it was.

In a final reply, Mr. Boyle wrote that Jeff had assured him that he was "under control." According to Boyle, Jeff was "desirous of getting back into the community." Jeff had told him that he had lined up an alcohol treatment program, and that he would "never, ever get in trouble again." In general, Boyle said, he found Jeff's current attitude "very positive." He acknowledged that I doubted Jeff's ability to control himself, or even to follow through on any treatment program in which he was not closely supervised. He even said that, "It may very well be that you are right in the final analysis," but his job was to get Jeff all that he was entitled to under the law, in this case, "consideration by the Court for his early release." And on that final note, Boyle concluded, "I must say thank you, and goodbye."

After that, I had no recourse but to go directly to the Court. On March 1, 1990, I wrote Judge Gardner a letter concerning my fears for Jeff, and for those he might injure if he were released before his alcoholism had been effectively treated. I went over the fact that Jeff had avoided therapeutic intervention in the past, and that even when he had been treated, it had been under the direction of a therapist who was not specialized in treating alcoholics, and that no reports about his progress, or lack of progress, had been made either to the Court or the Office of Probation and Parole.

"I have tremendous reservations about Jeff's chances when he hits the street," I told Judge Gardner. "I sincerely hope that you might intervene in some way to help my son whom I love very much and for whom I want a better life." I told the judge that I had heard of a treatment program that claimed great success in rehabilitating alcoholics and that Jeff's placement in a similarly rigorous program was critical to his future. "I do feel that this may be our last chance to institute something lasting," I wrote in the last line of my letter, "and that you can hold the key."

At the end of February 1990, I learned that Jeff was going to be released early from the Milwaukee County House of Correction, having served only ten months of his twelve-month sentence. He would be on probation for the next few years, but other than occasional visits to his probation officer, Jeff would be completely free.

Jeff was freed the following month. He moved back into my mother's house in West Allis, but there was no question that he could remain there indefinitely. She was old and increasingly frail, so it was necessary for Jeff to find a place of his own.

He found it in the Oxford Apartments on North Twenty-fifth Street. His apartment number was 213, and it was duly approved by Jeff's probation officer.

During the Thanksgiving holiday of 1990, Shari and I visited Jeff's new apartment. We found it exceedingly neat and orderly. It was furnished sparsely, a beige couch and chair supplied by the landlord. The kitchen and living room were combined, and Jeff proudly opened the refrigerator door to display how clean it was inside. The only thing odd about the kitchen was that he had bought a freezer.

"Why'd you buy that?" I asked.

"To save money," Jeff answered. "When there's a sale, I can stock up on things."

If anything, this struck me as a sensible idea, and I continued on my tour.

A short corridor led to the bathroom and bedroom, and it was cut off from the living room by a sliding door. Jeff had put a lock on that door, as if to seal it off completely.

"Why the lock?" I asked.

"Just to make it safer," Jeff answered. "Against burglars."

We all walked through the corridor and into the bedroom. There were a couple of black floor lamps, a television, and a computer.

"It looks good, Jeff," I said.

He smiled proudly.

On the way back to the living room, Shari stepped into the bathroom and pulled back the shower curtain. Two black towels hung neatly over a spotless bathtub.

A month later, during the Christmas holidays, I returned to Jeff's apartment a second time. Dave had come to West Allis with me this time, and I wanted to show him Jeff's apartment. Jeff walked us both through the apartment, and it appeared more or less unchanged from my first visit, except for the elaborate security system he'd set up for his protection. There was a camera mounted above the door and a host of alarms which, Jeff said, would make an "earth-shattering" sound should someone break into the apartment.

"You've got a lot of security," I told him.

He seemed to cast about for an explanation. "Well," he said finally, "there are a lot of robberies around here, and I don't want anyone to break in."

On Thanksgiving Day, 1990, Shari and I drove up to West Allis to spend the weekend with my mother. Jeff was scheduled to join us there, but he was very late. While we waited, I took out the video camera and filmed a short conversation with my mother. When it was over, she took me on a tour of the house, smiling a little shyly as the camera recorded her progress. She pointed out various rooms, then led me down into the basement. While she spoke, I let the camera pan along the far walls, past shelves of stored goods, and even a door beneath the stairs, one which was still as tightly closed as it had been months before when I had gone down into the basement to search for some clue as to the strange odors that had been continually rising into the main house. There were no odors that day. There had been no odors for quite some time. They had gone with Jeff.

Jeff arrived toward the middle of Saturday afternoon. He was dressed very neatly, his hair freshly combed. He wore large glasses, and a cloth jacket which he refused to take off even though the house was very warm. "No, no, I'll just leave it on," he kept saying, "I'll have to go out for a smoke soon anyway."

I took up the camera again, and made a videotape of my son. Through the lens I saw a handsome young man who slouched in the large stuffed chair only a few feet from me.

He smiled several times and talked about his new-found interest in aquarium fish. He answered my questions politely, and at one point, even got down on the floor and played with my mother's orange tabby. He seemed to have his life under control.

Now, when I look at that video, I see much more than I could possibly have seen before. In the chair,

Jeff sits with one leg over the other, a single foot dangling in midair. At each mention of his apartment, his foot twitches slightly. With each mention that I or someone else in the family may drop by to pay him a visit, it twitches. With each mention of what he is doing now, of how his job is going, of what he does in his spare time—it twitches. Something in his distant, half-dead gaze says, "If you only knew."

On July 22, 1991, I called Jeff's apartment several times. My mother had called to tell me that she had been unable to reach him, and that he had missed a promised visit to her house. The next morning, July 23, 1991, I called Jeff's apartment at about nine in the morning. The phone rang several times before someone finally answered it. At the other end I heard a man's voice, but it wasn't Jeff's.

"Is Jeff there?" I asked.

"Jeffrey Dahmer?" the man asked.

"That's right."

"No, he's not here right now," the man said in a guarded voice, as if he was being cautious about something.

"Where is Jeff?" I asked.

"He's not here," the man repeated, still speaking very guardedly. "Who is this?"

"I'm Jeff's father."

I could hear something catch in his breath. "You're Jeffrey Dahmer's father?"

"Yes," I told him. "Where is Jeff?"

"Well, your son's not here right now."

"Where is he?"

"Someone will call you, Mr. Dahmer."

"Call me? What about?"

"A detective will call you."

"A detective?" I repeated, thinking now that Jeff had probably gotten into trouble again, perhaps because he was drunk, or worse, that he had molested yet another child.

"What are you talking about?" I asked.

It was then that the man on the other end of the line finally told me who he was, that he was a member of the Milwaukee Police Department. He hesitated just an instant, then let the hammer fall. "We're investigating a homicide, Mr. Dahmer," he said.

"A homicide?" I asked, and suddenly I thought that I was about to receive what I felt at that time must surely be the worst news a parent could ever receive, that someone had murdered his child.

"Homicide?" I repeated. "You mean Jeff's been—"

"No, not Jeff," the man told me quickly, my son's name sounding like something dirty he did not want on his tongue. "Jeff is alive and well."

PART II

Many months after Jeff had already been sent to prison, and at the end of a long day of work, I decided to take a break by going to a movie. Shari and I picked out the film more or less at random, flipping through the local paper until we came upon an advertisement that seemed to suggest that this particular movie might be somewhat more relaxing than the usual fare. The ad pictured a lovely mountain scene. There was a sparkling stream in a wooded valley, and in the middle of the stream, a solitary boy was fly-fishing, his line thrust in a wide arc over the water. The name of the movie was *A River Runs Through It*.

As it turned out, the movie was about a wayward son, a smart, nice-looking boy who goes astray despite the best efforts of those who loved him, particularly his brother and his parents. On two occasions during the movie, characters make the point, very significantly, that the tragedy of life is that it is the people who are closest to us whom we cannot seem to reach.

Sitting obliviously, watching the screen, munching popcorn, it never struck that this dreadful truth applied to me. Later, when the connection was pointed out, I could not even remember the specific scenes, and certainly I had no thought that the movie's wayward son might represent Jeff, or that the hapless father might be me.

We came home from the movie and prepared for bed. The light on the answering machine was blinking, so I turned it on to receive the messages. One of them was a typical crank call, the sort I had grown accustomed to receiving. In this case, it was a teenage boy who, in his best horror-movie voice, warned, "I'm Jeffrey Dahmer and I'm coming home for the weekend."

The other message was from a woman. It was a voice that I recognized because of its distinctive southern accent. This particular woman had called quite a few times before, always desperately seeking information about Jeff. Shari and I had always refused to talk to her, but she had persisted. "You know who I am," she said that night in a voice that was eerily pleading. "Please, pick up."

No one had been home to pick up, nor would we have answered her if we had been home. Because of that, she continued in a soft, ghostly litany: "Please pick up. Please pick up. Please pick up. Please pick up." It continued for nearly a minute, a voice echoing in my living room, begging me to "pick up."

But I could not pick up. And I don't mean simply the phone. In a broader sense, I could not "pick up" on anything that tied me to Jeff in any way other than the one I had already accepted, that biologically, I was his father, and that I would continue to do my duty toward him as best I could. I would visit him in prison, and accept his phone calls on the weekend. I would send him a little money from time to time, so that he could buy a few things which the prison did not supply. I would handle whatever small problems he might have. I would try to be encouraging, try to help him make the most of his life. By then, these few simple things were what my fatherhood had been reduced to, a set of routine and relatively undemanding tasks.

And so, as I've come to realize—though in some cases I did not realize it until many months after Jeff's trial and imprisonment—I still could not face the deeper and most frightening elements of my relationship to my son. I was still baffled by his acts, but I had no desire to dwell upon them. Certainly, I felt no obligation to do so.

As to Jeff, himself, I still could not envision him in his murderousness. But neither did I make any effort whatsoever to do that. In fact, my mind almost never returned to that part of his life. Instead, when I thought of him at all, it was as a lively little boy, frozen in his innocence, safely positioned in the distant past.

But even when I thought of him as a man, a prisoner, a murderer, it seemed to me that my son was very far away from me. He was far away in the distance that physically separated us, and which was obvious; but he was also far away in his character and personality, which, it seemed to me, was no less obvious. In both of these senses, he was where I wanted him. Safely away. Far, far away.

For the darker side of my parenthood was still beyond my grasp.

Jeff, age fourteen, hamming for the camera at the swimming hole

CHAPTER EIGHT

At midmorning on July 23, I called my mother in West Allis to let her know that I had made contact with Jeff, and that something had clearly happened to him. I did not know exactly what had happened, but I knew with certainty that he was in some kind of trouble. I told her that a Milwaukee police officer had answered the phone when I'd called Jeff's apartment. I added that this same police officer had told me that he was investigating a homicide, but that he'd refused to tell me anything more. Instead, he had instructed me to wait for a later call.

To my astonishment, my mother informed me that the Milwaukee police were at her house at that very moment, and that they were searching it thoroughly, moving up and down the basement stairs and intently going through everything in Jeff's room.

"Why?" I asked. "What are they looking for?"

My mother did not know.

"Didn't they tell you anything?" I asked.

My mother seemed dazed, her reply unclear. It was obvious that she knew no more than I did about what the police were actually looking for as they roamed through her house, or even what kind of crime they were investigating.

One thing was clear to me instantly, however. If the police were investigating a homicide, and Jeff was still alive, then it was possible that he was also the person they were investigating. At that point, and for the first time, I began to consider the possibility that my son was not after all the victim of a crime, not one who had been murdered, but a murderer.

It was a possibility which was confirmed almost immediately. A police officer, Deputy Chief Robert Dues of the West Allis Police Department, came on the line. He introduced himself, and asked who I was. I told him, and then he informed me that he'd not told my mother everything about the case because he had found her, in his words, "rather overwhelmed."

"What's happening over there?" I asked. "What exactly are you doing?"

"We're conducting a homicide investigation with the Milwaukee Police Department."

"But Jeff doesn't live with my mother."

"Yes, I know."

"So this investigation, it involves Jeff?"

"Yes, it does."

"You mean, you think that he may have murdered somebody?"

"That's what we're investigating, yes."

Despite the fact that such a possibility had quickly entered my mind only seconds before, I was nonetheless stunned by the abruptness of the policeman's reply. For a moment, I was not fully able even to register the full gravity of what had just been said to me.

"And so, Jeff has been arrested?" I asked.

"Yes, he has."

"For murder?"

"I'm afraid so, Mr. Dahmer."

Had Deputy Chief Dues told me that my son had been murdered, I might have had a sudden vision of him as a murder victim, dead at the hands of someone else, his body sprawled in an alley or a bedroom or some vague landscape my mind quickly imagined. Knowing Jeff as I did, I would have been able to accept such a possibility far more quickly. His shyness, his passivity, his low self-esteem, all of these things made him fit the role of victim far better than any other I might have imagined in a murder scenario. His new apartment was not in a very safe neighborhood, and I knew that he'd already been mugged. It would have been easy for me to imagine him coming home late at night, perhaps drunk and staggering, a ready target for a mugging. I also knew that in the past Jeff had become abusive while drunk, and in a mugging situation, such behavior could have easily ended in his death.

But I had been told something else altogether, that

my son had murdered someone else. Easy as it would have been to imagine him murdered, I found it impossible to imagine him as a murderer, a dark, hulking figure wielding a knife or a gun. The Jeff I'd known was far too soft-spoken, generally passive, and slow to anger. I saw him only as the type of person who could easily be thought of as a hapless victim. In a murderous scenario, I could imagine him in no other role.

I called Shari right away, but she was not in her office. As it turned out, I would not be able to reach her for at least two hours. In the meantime, I called Gerald Boyle. He had previously represented Jeff in the child molestation case, and I thought that he might have some information about the investigation.

I found Boyle quite excited.

"Lionel, I've been trying to reach you," he said. "People have been calling me all morning."

"What people?"

"Media people. The press."

"Media people? What do they want?"

"They're trying to find out everything about Jeff."

"What about Jeff? What's going on? Nobody's given me any details."

"I got a call from the police," Mr. Boyle continued. "Jeff has been arrested for attempted murder."

I was confused, even a bit relieved. Attempted murder was far less serious than murder. Perhaps the policeman at my mother's house had gotten it all wrong.

But it was a relief that quickly disappeared. Hastily, in short, clipped sentences, Boyle described a situation that did not in the least add up to a charge of attempted murder. It was clear he had simply misspoken, and that Jeff had not "attempted" murder, but accomplished it.

"They've found body parts in Jeff's apartment," he said. "A lot of them. Different people."

"Different?"

"More than one person," Boyle said. "We don't know how many. It could be three or more. The police found several IDs in Jeff's apartment, too. Young adults, evidently." For a moment, he seemed staggered by the very information he was giving me. "I can't believe this is the same Jeff I know. Have you ever talked to his parole officers?"

"Yes."

"They didn't pick up that he might do any of this?"

"Not that I know of."

Boyle sounded incredulous, but moved quickly on to the next point. "Well, give me another hour, and I'll try to get more information from the police."

Boyle called several times during the next two hours, but he was not able to shed any more light on Jeff's situation. Thus, when I finally reached Shari, I had no more information than I'd had hours before.

I had already talked to Shari once. It had been earlier that same morning, directly after talking to the policeman in Jeff's apartment. We had both agreed that Jeff was probably in trouble again for molestation, a serious charge, but nothing like the one which appeared to confront him now.

"The police are investigating Jeff for homicide," I told her.

It was so far from Shari's mind that my son could possibly have been involved in a murder, that she said, "Suicide? Jeff's tried to commit suicide?"

"No," I said, this time more slowly. "Homicide."

Then I added the only detail that could possibly have been more shocking. "More than one. At least three."

Three.

Three murders.

At least.

What does a father do with such information?

I did what I had always done. I collapsed into a strange silence that was neither angry nor sullen nor sorrowful, but just a silence, a numbness, a terrible, inexpressible emptiness. Overwhelmed and unable to deal with the thoughts that whirled through my mind, I mechanically returned to the routine task I'd been doing just before the call to my mother, in this case, editing analysis methods for silica. Dutifully, carefully, with the deepest concentration, I focused on matters of chemical methodology.

This is not to say that my mind was not reeling with all that my son might have done, all the unanswered questions of his crimes, or even with the bizarre vision of scores of police officials swarming about my mother's house, but only that I compulsively returned to what remained stable and predictable in my life, the old refuge of the laboratory.

Throughout that long afternoon, I told no one about what had happened to Jeff. Instead, I simply labored to maintain my calm, to act as if nothing had happened. All around me, my associates were laughing and joking and going about their normal routines. My office mate talked about some analytical report sheets, whether or not those particular samples had been completed. I answered his questions with the sturdy professionalism that seemed, at that point, the one indisputably reliable feature of my life.

For the next few hours, my inner world took on the sinister atmosphere of a dark and desperately guarded secret. It was not a feeling that was new to me, however, but one which, over the years, I had grown accustomed to. In 1988, when Jeff had been arrested for child molestation, I had kept it a secret. I had also kept secret all the other things I had learned after that. I had kept Jeff's earlier arrest for indecent exposure a secret. I had kept his homosexuality a secret, his addiction to pornography, his theft of a department-store manikin, everything a secret. Without knowing it, a kind of secrecy had begun to entomb my life, turning the deepest part of it into a basement hiding place.

Now this most secret, guarded, and fiercely protected life was about to be exploded. The very notion of such sudden, terrible, and deeply personal exposure worked to keep me in a state of incomprehensible denial.

It was not total denial, however. For example, I did not at any point think that the phone was going to ring suddenly and someone was going to say "April Fool, it's all a joke." Instead, I labored to minimize the awesome information which had suddenly come to me. I allowed myself to believe that although Jeff might be implicated in a homicide, he was not the actual murderer. I accepted the fact that perhaps someone had, indeed, been killed in Jeff's apartment, but I insisted on the notion that the murder might not have been committed by Jeff. Perhaps my son had been framed, set up, I thought. Perhaps all the evidence against him was merely circumstantial. Perhaps Jeff had only found the bodies, and because of that accidental discovery, had been hurled into the center of a series of murders he'd had nothing to do with. Desperately, I tried to keep my son in the role of victim, someone who had haplessly gotten ensnared in a net of terrible circumstances.

Such conjectures lifted my mind into a state of unreal and dreamy suspension. I literally felt myself hanging above my life, above Jeff's life, above everything but the minute laboratory tasks I continued to pursue with a ferocious intensity. But even as I worked, I was sometimes hit by hot rushes, as if I were being periodically given injections of antihistamines or niacin, waves of heat rushing over my chest and head. It was as if my body had begun to send its own distress signals, warning my mind that it could not forever keep the truth at bay.

But which truth? The truth that my son was a murderer? Or the truth that my life was tied to his, sinking in the same quicksand?

Terrible as it seems to me now, I know that my essential emotional response that first horrible day was based upon a fear of being personally exposed, my life wholly and nakedly revealed, and the excruciating embarrassment that such a process would cause me. Jeff had hit bottom as a son, absolute bottom, and I could feel that he was taking me down with him, dragging me into the utter chaos that he had made of his life, and doing it publicly.

Throughout that endless afternoon, this deep, personal dread built steadily in me. To avoid it, I continued to concentrate on my laboratory work. I completed task after routine task, my mind completely focused on the details, as if by such absolute and exclusive concentration, I could keep avoiding the frightening disorder that had suddenly overwhelmed the other part of my life, the one I rigidly controlled.

Even though I was racing at my top speed, I did not stop working until around seven-thirty. I had no choice but to complete endless loose ends and brief my supervisor before I left for a stay in Milwaukee of unknown length.

At one point on the long drive home, I stopped at one of the rest stops along the Pennsylvania-Ohio Turnpike and called Shari. She told me that she'd been able to get me onto the early morning flight to Milwaukee instead of the one scheduled for later that night. I was relieved, because I wanted to gain some mental equilibrium with Shari before going on to the unknown horrors in Milwaukee. My mind was in a suspended, unreal state, a play of whirling, disconnected images. More than anything, I found myself replaying my son's life. I saw him again as an infant, then as a small child playing with his dog. I saw him as a young boy, riding his bicycle. I saw his eyes as we'd released the bird. I wanted to take him back to that early boyhood time, to freeze him there, so that he could never reach beyond the innocence and harmlessness of his childhood, never reach any of the people whose lives he had destroyed . . . never reach me.

Each time I thought of the older Jeff, I pushed him aside, shut him up in a closet, smothered him in the darkness, where he sat, alone, with whatever it was he had done. I did not even want to consider the things he might have done, or in any way bring them to mind. At the very thought of murder, my mind closed down or shifted to the side, a maneuver that I would be using for months to come.

*   *   *

Shari was at home when I arrived. She had gotten home around seven-thirty. A sheriff's patrol car had been waiting for her, and she had immediately asked the three men, two sheriff's deputies and a captain, into the house. The captain, with great concern, had introduced himself, then asked her if she was Jeff's mother. Shari had replied that she was his stepmother, and that she was already aware that Jeff had been arrested. The captain told my wife that he and his men were there to help us in any way they could, and would be only a phone call away.

When I got home, Shari told me about all these things, and for the first time, the eeriness of our situation, the sheer enormity of the change that had suddenly overcome our lives, settled in upon us.

We were no longer merely parents, and we never would be again. We were the parents, and I, in particular, was the father of Jeffrey Dahmer. Jeffrey, not Jeff. Jeffrey Dahmer was someone else, the formal public name for a man who was, at least to me, still Jeff, still my son. Even my son's name had become public property, foreign to me, a press report's designation, the name of a stranger, an abrupt depersonalization of someone who, at least to me, was still incontestably a person.

That night, I began to feel the weight of my son's public identity more powerfully than at any time before. Turning on the eleven o'clock news, I sat in my living room and saw my son's face fill the screen. Switching from channel to channel, I saw that same face flash before me again and again, along with other photographs and news videos, pictures of his apartment building, of men with masks removing vats, an enormous blue drum, and a squat kitchen freezer. I saw them take out the refrigerator he had so casually opened for our inspection the day we'd visited his apartment. Only this time, it was being lugged down a flight of stairs and hauled into a police van. I saw hordes of officials as they swarmed in and out of a building whose significance to me had been, before that night, merely casual. In other photographs and videos, these same legions lingered outside my mother's house in West Allis, filing in and out of its front and side doors with a sense of ownership and authority which could only strike me as surreal.

Sitting beside me, Shari stared unbelievingly at the television screen, shocked at the images she saw, unnerved by their intrusiveness, but already beginning to sink into a new, radically altered reality. I could feel her tension, and tried to relieve it.

"Maybe some day this will all be over," I told her.

Her reply was gently direct "This will never be over, Lionel," she said.

She was right, and as I continued to watch the news that night, Jeff's face flashing before me again and again, I should have known that. Only the weekend before, we had gone to St. Louis on a business trip, stopping to visit Dave in Cincinnati on the way. Dave's neighborhood was made up of large Victorian houses, and that evening, we had taken a long walk through it. From the streets we'd seen people lounging on their large porches, talking quietly, enjoying the warm summer night. The peace had been very sweet.

In St. Louis the next day, we had gone to a birthday party, mingling with friends and a few of Shari's friends and business associates. We had stayed at the Holiday Inn, and, strange as it seems now, we had signed the register in our own names.

That occasion was the last time we were able to feel safe in doing such an open, ordinary thing as signing our own names innocently and without fear on a hotel register five hundred miles from our home. That part of life, its casual anonymity, had suddenly been wrenched from us. We were about to become public figures, and we would never be anything else. For as surely as Jeff had become "Jeffrey," we were to become "the Dahmers."

The next morning I took a 7:00 A.M. flight to Milwaukee. Once in the city, my friends Dick and Tom Jungck picked me up and drove me to the Wisconsin Club to meet Gerald Boyle. Boyle assured me that he would stay on the case, and that his assistant was with Jeff at that moment, taking down his statement. He told me that he had already scheduled a press conference for that afternoon, and that he wanted me to stand at his side when he gave it.

It was no doubt a normal request, a show of support between a father and his son, but I refused. I was still guarding my privacy, my right to remain obscure, a figure on the sidelines. I was also guarding my pride, whatever reputation I had fought for as a man, a father, a husband. I cringed at the prospect of standing beside my son's lawyer, of being gawked at by reporters, of having their lights shining in my face. To give up so much of my privacy as a person was simply impossible for me. I was simply too shy, too shocked, to unsure of what I actually felt to stand in a public place and declare that I was *Jeffrey* Dahmer's father.

It is clear to me now that I was still trying, as much as possible, to protect my own and my family's name from the enormous embarrassment and shame that had suddenly fallen upon it. My mother, now in her eighties, had lived an upright and honest life. She had never harmed anyone, and I did not want her to see my face on a television broadcast, see me standing mutely before the cameras, a public spectacle, broken and pitiful and helpless. Because my son had brought her name into public disgrace, I felt duty-bound to keep at least that part of it that was still mine, and which I could still to some extent control, out of the glare of the public arena, beyond its rage and scorn.

And so, a few hours later, when Boyle stepped before the cameras, surrounded by scores of newspaper and television reporters to declare that my son was anguished and remorseful, to admit, at least figuratively, that he was lost, lost, lost, I was not there to be pointed out, to be questioned, or even to be held up as an example of suffering and devoted fatherhood.

I have since come to understand that at that time—and perhaps it is my doom to be so forever—I was a creature of consciously selected roles. Rather than having developed a natural fatherhood, I had learned, as if by rote, what a father should do. He should provide physical support. He should give advice. He should take his son to the fishing hole. To some extent, I had learned the same behaviors as regards my obligations as a son. I should visit my mother. I should call her on the telephone. I should send her a birthday card. Both as father and as son, I was the player of a well-learned part.

Up until that day in July, when Boyle asked me to stand before the world and declare my fatherly devotion, I had never experienced any deep conflict in these two fundamental and irreducible roles. I could play father and son with equal alacrity, the beauty of the one performance enhancing the beauty of the other. But suddenly, the roles had come into conflict, become intersecting rather than parallel lines of behavior. My role as father demanded that I stand with Boyle. My role as son, as guardian of my family's name, demanded that I not.

It would be infinitely pleasant for me to believe that I made my choice based upon a recognizably human criteria, that love or devotion, gratitude or tenderness played some part in my decision. But they did not. I do not even know exactly how I came to decide that I would not stand by Boyle at the press conference that afternoon. Perhaps my sense of the futility of such an appearance played some part, the realization that Jeff was well beyond the salutary effects of such a paltry demonstration. My feeling of the futility of doing it was enforced by Dick and Tom's echoing of the same sentiment when they picked me up after my meeting with Boyle. Or perhaps some part of my brain flipped a coin, and it came down on the side of my role as son.

In any event, I did not go to the press conference that afternoon, but to Tom's house, where, after a sympathetic review of the day's events, I walked into the bedroom, lay down, and went to sleep. And so I did not even see the press conference. I preferred a brief oblivion, instead.

*　　*　　*

Although I could avoid a press conference, I could not avoid the matters with which it had dealt, or the fact that Jeff's crimes had become a sensational news event.

Around 3:30 P.M., my friends drove me to my mother's house in West Allis. I felt that I needed to explain what Jeff had done, as well as to protect her from harassment. Two reporters had already taken up positions across the street from her house, their camcorders on tripods, so I decided to pass the house, then turn into the alley that ran behind it. Dick spotted another reporter stationed in the alley, however, so he went past the reporter and stopped in a blocking position to allow me to jump out and race through the backyard and through the side door of the house.

I found my mother in her recliner, resting silently in the living room. She looked relieved to see me.

"Oh, it's you," she said.

During the next few minutes, I told her that I had seen Jeff's lawyer, had arranged for his defense, and that I had now come to protect her from what was likely to be a great deal of unwanted intrusion.

"I've seen some things on T.V.," my mother said, still baffled by the flurry of police activity that had swirled through her house over the last two days. Her mind remained locked in the past, her memories of Jeff disconnected from the most immediate events.

"When I saw Jeff," she said, "he looked thin. He looked pale." She appeared highly stressed, confused, her mind unable to grasp the enormity of what Jeff had done. My son's pallid and emaciated appearance constituted a defense in her mind, evidence that so weak a man could not have carried out so strenuous an act as murder.

I glanced out the front window, spotted the two reporters across the street, and pulled the blinds. For a long time, my mother and I sat in the shadowy silence of that curtained room. My mother continued to talk, almost obsessively, as if by talking, she could get a hold on what my son had done. But her mind was fuzzy, vague, disordered, and the more she tried to get a grip on the events that had recently swept over her, the more the ultimate horror of them eluded her. It was like the dreadful opposite of a rainbow, a nightmare which, as she moved toward it, receded from her grasp.

For the next half hour, my mother and I continued to sit quietly in the front room. There were moments when it almost felt as if nothing had happened, or could ever happen, that would be able to disturb our peace.

But that was an illusion, of course, and we were only able to dwell in it for a short time. For by 4:30 P.M., other reporters had begun to arrive, joining the small contingent that was already there. After that, they descended upon my mother's house in a steady, and continually widening, stream. They came in cars, in vans, and sometimes on foot. They brought cameras, tripods, microphones, notebooks. They trampled flowers and bushes. They rang the doorbell so insistently that I took down the chimes. They knocked so loudly at the door that they rattled its window panes. Their calls kept the telephone ringing continually, so that I finally disconnected it. They peeked in the windows and rummaged around the house and garage. They yelled at us and at each other, their voices a continual disruption to our conversation.

To me, this was a terribly frightening intrusion, but to my mother, it was incomprehensible. She had lived her life as one who opened her door at someone's knock, who answered the phone when it rang. She found it nearly impossible not to do those things. At each intrusion, she would react as if it were the first she had experienced. Unable directly to associate the commotion she observed around her with Jeff's crimes, she continually sought the reason for it. Repeatedly, I told her that the people gathered around her house were only re   rters, that they were harmless people who were only doing their jobs. It was Jeff they wanted, I told her. It had nothing to do with her.

Lost in her own hazy consciousness, my mother found such explanations unacceptable. Since she had only allowed herself the vaguest understanding of Jeff's crimes, she could not connect the frenzy on her lawn with anything he had done. No matter how often I tried to explain it to her, she always renewed her questions. "Who are they? What do they want? What's that noise?" No answer could satisfy her, and with each attempt, her bewilderment deepened, until, by nightfall, she seemed to drift in and out of consciousness, her eyes darting about, almost fearfully, like an animal caught in a grave and inescapable confusion.

By around nine that night, the reporters finally began to drift away, and in the ensuing and welcome quiet, I decided to play a game of double solitaire with my mother. I had played this game with her both as a child and as a young man, and it had always appeared to relax her. She smiled brightly when I suggested it, so I escorted her delicately to her bedroom, and we sat down on her bed and began to play.

For the next few minutes, a great quietness settled over us, and some of the childlike fear and anxiety that had marked my mother's face during the evening began to release its grip.

We were well into our third hand when I suddenly heard a scattering of hard, metallic pops. They were very loud, and at first I thought that a barrage of stones had been hurled at the front of the house by people who were getting back at Jeff by attacking us. Either that, or something worse, gunshots.

I rushed my mother into another bedroom, away from the front of the house, and told her to stay there. Then I ran to the living room and called the police. After that, I waited beside the front window and carefully looked out. The street was dark. There was no traffic. There were no more popping sounds.

When the police arrived, I stepped out into the yard. I saw nothing in the street or along the sidewalk, but when I turned back to the house, I saw that its front white aluminum siding was dented in various spots, and that it was dripping with egg yoke in at least a dozen places.

There was nothing to do but rinse it off, so with the police still present, I pulled the hose into the front yard and washed the front of the house.

A short time later, at around eleven that night, I returned my mother to her room, and put her to bed. I will never forget the confusion in her face, the sense of vulnerability, the darkness that gathered in her eyes, her fear.

"It was just eggs," I told her.

She stared at me uncomprehendingly. "Eggs?"

"Someone threw eggs at the house," I told her.

"Why?" she asked.

There was no way I could explain it all to her.

"Just eggs, Mom," I repeated. Then I got up and headed for the door.

Once at the door, I turned back and looked at her. "Good night," I said.

She offered a slight, but still confused, smile. "Sleep well, my dear son," she said just before I turned out the light.

It did not seem possible that I ever would.

155

Lionel's parents bending over to inspect Lionel's
prize tomato plants, student housing, Ames, Iowa,
1963

CHAPTER NINE

T he next morning, my friends picked me up and drove me to the Wisconsin Club, where I met Boyle. The two of us then went to the Safety Building, which, along with the Sheriff's Department and various courtrooms, housed the Milwaukee County Jail, where Jeff was being held. On the way, Boyle told me that Jeff had made some statements indicating that he might commit suicide, and consequently, he had been placed on suicide watch.

Once at the Safety Building, Boyle and one of his assistants escorted me into a stark room, its walls painted light yellow, and with a long bench and table. For a while I sat, more or less silently, while Boyle and his assistant worked on various papers, their backs to me, trying to give me as much privacy as possible.

Jeff arrived a few minutes later. In all the days of his alcoholism, in the deepest moments of his long descent, I had never seen him look so utterly haggard, so weak, so broken, so lost. Handcuffed, unshaven, his hair uncombed, his body draped in loose-fitting prison garb, he came into the room like some character in a cheap prison drama.

He showed no emotion when he caught sight of me. He did not smile or offer the slightest sense of welcome. "I guess I've really done it this time," was all he said. Then, once again, in what had become the refrain of a life lived as one long apology, he said, "I'm sorry."

I stepped forward, put my arms around him and began to cry. While I held him, Jeff stood in place, still showing no emotion.

"How's Grandma?" he asked as I released him.

It was then that we began a conversation that was utterly typical of us in its featurelessness, in the clipped phrases we used, the whole array of quick evasions by which we slipped into triviality, and by that means, refused to confront the gravity our lives had taken on, the fact that we were both now riding on a nightmare wave.

"She's doing OK," I told him. "She sends her love."

He looked as if he felt he did not deserve it.

"I'm really sorry for all the trouble I've caused her," he said.

"Well, she's going to be all right," I told him. "We've had some trouble at the house, though. There were a lot of reporters around, that sort of thing."

"So they're really bothering you?"

"They have been, yeah. We had some eggs thrown at the house."

He stared at me blankly.

I stared at him blankly.

"The police are helping us," I added after a moment. "They do the best they can."

"Well, maybe all the reporters will go away after a while."

"Maybe."

There was a long silence, neither of us speaking, then Jeff nodded briefly, expressionlessly, a nod that was little more than a twitch.

"The roses look good," I told him, "the ones you planted."

"That's good."

"The yellow ones and the red ones."

"That's good. It's a nice garden."

"The cat's doing fine. She always wants to be brushed."

Jeff nodded.

"You know how she likes that."

"Yeah."

"She's always trying to be brushed," I said. "Remember how you used to do it?"

He stared at me silently.

I shrugged, and added nothing else.

"I don't know what to say," Jeff said finally.

"I don't either."

"I really screwed up this time."

"Yes, you did."

"I really blew it."

"Well, you can still be treated, Jeff," I told him. "I didn't really realize how sick you were."

Jeff said nothing.

"You need help, Jeff."

"I guess," he said flatly.

"We just need to make sure you get some help."

He nodded.

"You know, mental help."

"I guess so."

"Maybe you can get better, Jeff."

"Maybe."

"With professionals, people who can help you."

Jeff seemed hardly to hear me. "How's Shari?" he asked, though without interest.

"Fine."

"Good."

"She sends her love."

"Good."

"She's at home in Ohio."

"She didn't come up?"

"No, not yet."

He fell silent for a few seconds, then suddenly blurted, "The food is bad in here."

"It is?"

"And it's hard to sleep. There's a lot of screaming."

160

"Well, just do your best," I told him.

"They keep the lights on all the time."

"Well, try to sleep."

"OK."

"You need to sleep."

He thought a moment, as if going over the events of the last few days, then he rolled his eyes up toward the ceiling. "I really messed up."

"Yes, but Shari and I will stand by you, Jeff."

"Sorry," he said again, but with that same deadness and lack of emotion. He did not seem to comprehend the enormous consequences of what he had done. "Sorry," he repeated.

Sorry?

But for what?

For the men he had killed?

For the anguish of their relatives?

For the torment of his grandmother?

For the ruin of his own family?

There was no way to tell exactly what Jeff was sorry for.

It was at that precise moment that I actually glimpsed the full character of my son's madness, saw it physically, as if it were a scar across his face.

It was impossible to tell whom he felt sorry for, or what he felt sorry about. He could not even imitate regret, much less truly feel it. Remorse was beyond him, and he could probably sense it only as an emotion felt by people in another galaxy. He was beyond

161

the call of a role, incapable of acting a part. His "Sorry" was a mummified remain, an artifact retained from that distant time when he'd still been able to sense, if only to imitate, a normal range of feeling.

Suddenly, I thought of Jeff's childhood, and his general remoteness no longer looked like shyness, but like disconnection, the opening of an unbridgeable abyss. His eyes no longer struck me merely as expressionless, but as utterly void, beyond the call of the most basic forms of sympathy and understanding, beyond even the capacity to ape such emotions. As he stood before me at that instant, my son, perhaps for the first time in his adult life, presented himself to me as he really was, destitute of feeling, his emotions shaved down to a bare minimum, a young man who was deeply, deeply ill, and for whom, in all likelihood, there was no way out.

Jeff will kill himself, I thought with a strange certainty. *No one can live like this.*

A few minutes later, Jeff was led away, still walking in the same rigid posture, his hands cuffed in front of him. *No one can live like this,* I repeated in my mind. And yet, in a sense, as I was increasingly to discover over the next few months, I, too, had lived like "this": a man who found it hard to express his emotions; who focused on the minutiae of social life and often lost track of its overall design; who relied on others to direct his responses to life because he could not trust his own sense of the way it really worked—a man whose son was perhaps only the deeper, darker shadow of himself.

After the meeting with Jeff, Boyle and I returned to the Wisconsin Club. During the drive, he told me that in his opinion, Jeff was insane, and that insanity was his only possible defense. He said that he already had a psychiatrist in mind, one who could conduct a thorough psychiatric examination of Jeff. He did not say in what way he thought my son was insane. He named no specific disorder. Such determination could only be arrived at through a vigorous psychiatric study, he said.

Clearly, it was not Boyle's intention to get Jeff off. The goal was to locate him in a psychiatric hospital, rather than a prison. In a hospital, Jeff would get considerably better psychiatric help than he would in prison, Boyle told me, and perhaps, at some point, he might actually become sane.

This sounded reasonable to me. Under no conditions would I have wanted Jeff to "get off." Although the full extent of his madness was still unknown to me, the man I'd just seen in the small yellow room at the Milwaukee County Jail was clearly insane. Any attempt to set him free, even if I had thought it possible, would have struck me as absurd.

At that point, I believed that it was my son's madness that most powerfully and permanently separated us. He lived in a world behind his eyes. I could never enter that world. We would always be separated by the barrier of his mental illness. In a sense, I saw nothing but his insanity.

There had been times in the past when I had said to myself, and sometimes to Shari, "He's crazy." I'd usually said it in anger and frustration, and I'd always meant that he was disordered, that he couldn't keep his life together or think his way out of things. It had never occurred to me that he might be thinking his way "in" to something, that during all the time when I had been so often concerned with Dave, or with my work at the lab, or with trying to get over my divorce, that my eldest son might have been going slowly insane.

But now, suddenly, I could see Jeff's insanity in everything about him. It was in his motionless face, in his dull eyes, in the hard rigidity of his body, in the way his arms did not sway back and forth when he walked, even in the expressionless way he muttered, "Sorry."

And of course, it was in his murderousness. But as I have since come to recognize, had it not been for his murderousness, had his insanity not finally emerged in the insanity of his crimes, I might never have seen it at all. Until Shari had found him drunk in his room,

I had not seen his alcoholism. Until my mother had discovered the stolen manikin in his closet, I had not thought him particularly odd, and certainly not a thief. Until a great deal of information had come to me after he'd been arrested for molesting a child, it had not occurred to me that he was a homosexual, despite the fact that he had never had a date, that he'd taken a "friend" to the prom, that during all the years of his young adulthood, he had never expressed the slightest interest in a woman. It was a level of obliviousness, or perhaps denial, that was scarcely imaginable, and yet it was real. It was as if I had locked my son in a soundproof booth, then drawn the curtains so that I could neither hear nor see what he had become.

And yet, even at that time, the extent of Jeff's crimes, the fact that he had murdered a great many people, could hardly have been more clear to me. But the deeply perverse nature of his murderousness, along with all the insane thoughts and fantasies which both preceded and followed the murders, still remained vague to me. For although much information, all of it incomprehensibly hideous, had emerged from Apartment 213, the full story of my son's crimes had not.

But even if I had known everything at this early stage, I'm not sure I would have been able to accept it. Although I had certainly accepted the fact that Jeff was a murderer, that he was both a sexual murderer

165

and a multiple murderer, nonetheless, some part of me could not go beyond these most recent and most horrendous admissions.

And so, some part of me shut down. I read the newspapers, I watched the newscasts, but I did not probe for more. I did not ask Boyle to keep me informed as to the details of the case. Nor did I ask the police to report on what their criminal investigations were uncovering. Some part of me did not want to know: the part that lingered in denial, minimized, and evaded; the part that, against all reason and the enormous weight of the evidence, still cried out, "Not Jeff."

Once I'd seen Jeff, I remained with my mother for a few days, then returned to Medina County, not far from Akron, where Shari and I were living in a condo in a spacious residential area. It was near her work, though distant from mine, so for the last few years, I had been spending the week at my job in Pittsburgh, then returning home for the weekend.

Once at home, Shari brought me up-to-date on all that had happened at home during the last few days. The same kind of media whirlwind that had swirled around my mother's house had swirled around this one, too. Reporters had staked themselves out at various places around the house. She'd continually heard her name called from the outside, reporters begging her for interviews. There had been no letup on these intrusions, the constant ringing at the door, the constant ringing of the telephone. In response, Shari had disconnected the doorbell and let the answering machine take our calls. For days, as she told me, she had felt like a trapped animal. It had gotten so bad that the Sheriff's Department had recommended that she leave the house, but she had refused. They had also recommended that she change her telephone number to one that was unlisted, but she had refused to do that, too.

"I will not be run out of my own house," she had told the sheriff's deputies.

During all that time, she added, only one neighbor had offered assistance. In all her life, she said, she had never felt more alone.

The fact that seemed hardest to understand was that we, ourselves, had done nothing to deserve such unwanted attention. But this was a fact that no longer mattered. Perhaps it had never mattered. We were the Dahmers. We had ceased to be anything else.

That night, we hardly spoke at all. It was as if each of us had been gutted. Drained, exhausted, still partly numb, we sat on the sofa and stared at the television. But as we both separately realized, even this light, generally relaxing activity, so common among ordinary people at the end of the working day, was now filled with extreme and unavoidable tension for us.

For at any moment, in the middle of comedy, at the tail end of drama, just before a commercial, we might suddenly see the face of my son, a face that I, at least, profoundly did not want to see.

Arriving home on Sunday, July 28, 1991, I had fully expected to return to work at the laboratory the next morning. Life had to go on, I thought, and certainly, given the projects that I had to put on hold in my rush to Milwaukee, I needed to get back to put them in some semblance of order.

But my return to the normalcy of work was not to be as easy as all that. On Sunday night, I'd called the personnel director at my job. He'd told me that a caravan of media trucks, complete with satellite disks, had shown up at the laboratory on Wednesday. They had taken up nearly the entire traffic circle. Fewer people had shown up the second day, but the director believed that it was better for me to remain at home. "Maybe you should stay in Ohio until we are sure it's all died down," he said.

And so, on that Monday morning, neither Shari nor I went to work. Instead, we stayed at home, listening to the incessant clangor of the phone, normally a welcome sound, or at least not an unwelcome one, but now a jarring one, as if it had become the single blunt instrument the whole world could use against us.

From the very beginning, the nature of the phone calls we received was very different from the nature of the letters that later began to pour in to us as well. Sometimes we received offers from people to use their homes as a refuge, along with messages of genuine sympathy or understanding. Usually, it was just the opposite. Often it was a television network, a newspaper, a magazine, all of them desperate for a story. On other occasions, it was a lawyer asking to represent Jeff, or a psychiatrist or psychologist seeking access to examine him. Rarely, it was something worse, people who had become obsessed with Jeff, who wanted to talk to him, to meet him.

Within days after Jeff's arrest, a single terrible aspect of his murders became obvious, the element of race.

From the beginning, it had been clear that almost all of Jeff's victims had been black, and this fact had made a great many people see him as a race-killer, someone who had purposely chosen black victims. Of all the charges that had been made against Jeff, this seemed to me the only one that absolutely was not true. My son had done terrible things, although at that time I didn't know just how terrible some of them had been, but his murders had not been racial murders. He had wanted bodies, muscular, male bodies. For me, it was as simple as that. The color of their skin hadn't mattered to him in the least.

There were many people who simply didn't believe this, however. They saw the faces of Jeff's victims, the fact that most of them were black, and drew their own conclusions. It was a conclusion that attracted a large number of people, even some celebrities, but it wasn't an idea I could accept. True, there were many, many things that I didn't know, and had never known, about Jeff. But I did know that he was insane. I had glimpsed that insanity, and I knew that his crimes had had nothing to do with race, and everything to do with madness. He had preyed upon young black men merely because they had been the easiest to prey upon. Many of them had been poor, and so they had needed the paltry fifty dollars he had offered them. Others had simply been available in the neighborhood, and he had taken advantage of the sheer convenience of having them near at hand. I saw Jeff's murders in precisely those terms, analytically, rather than emotionally.

But others saw his crimes quite differently, and in the following days, they held demonstrations and called for the firing of the police chief of Milwaukee, along with the officers who had, at various times, failed to capture Jeff.

The city appeared on the point of explosion, and as I watched the tension build in Milwaukee, it seemed inconceivable to me that anything so enormous could have been generated by my son. My mind recalled only a young man who was passive and more or less nondescript, a failure at almost everything he'd ever tried, a mixer in a chocolate factory, a job that placed him barely above a menial laborer. Now he was not only famous, but the catalyst for a thousand different reactions. All his life, he had been so very small, it seemed to me. There were times he'd been so small that I'd scarcely seen him at all. Now he was gigantic, the public personality around whom enormous forces swirled. How could this be the same Jeff who spoke in mumbled sentences, who'd sold blood for liquor, who'd muttered his characteristic, ''Sorry,'' at every offense, then slunk away, embarrassed and ashamed? How could so small and insignificant a man be blown up to such dimensions at such a blinding speed? How could so gray and unaccented and generally pathetic a figure generate such passion? Never had the vast gulf that separated what Jeff was and what he had done seemed so wide.

At that time, of course, it hardly occurred to me that Jeff was not alone in being transformed into a symbol, but that Shari and I were being put through the same process.

But as the days passed, both of us realized that we had also begun to take on larger-than-life qualities, that our lives had assumed an unexpected significance for a vast number of people whom we had never met and would never know.

For years, Shari and I had lived quietly near Medina, an ordinary couple who had gotten the same mail everyone else did, letters from relatives, advertisements, bills, even the occasional flyer that did not bother to give a name, but listed us only as "Occupants."

The anonymity of that kind of life had abruptly ended with Jeff's crimes. Only days after they had been revealed, and Jeff's face was plastered across every newspaper and television screen, almost any letter in Ohio that was addressed to "the Dahmers," and which gave no further directions, came to us. They began arriving almost from the very first days after Jeff's arrest. They came from all over the United States, and from several foreign countries. The vast majority were sympathetic, letters written by people who wanted us to know that they could feel our troubles, although, as they admitted, they could not imagine the extent of them. A few letters came from organizations, such as CURE, an association of people whose relatives are in prison. In general, they were letters of support, letters of advice.

But there was another kind of letter as well, letters that came from people who identified with us as parents whose lives had finally been consumed in the fire of parenthood, and who sympathized with our ordeal.

Poignantly, many were from other parents whose children had also gone terribly astray. Often, these letters began with, "I have a son," or "I have a daughter," and then went on to tell us of some child they no longer saw or talked to, a girl or boy who had slipped beyond their grasp, fallen into drugs or bad company or simple isolation, and never returned again. They encouraged us to stand by Jeff as they had stood by their children.

Shari read all of these letters, and I would often see her sitting alone, with piles of them scattered at her feet. I read very few, and even then, only those she kept out for me to read. I did not want to read them, and it was hard for me to understand why Shari did. I didn't want to feel for these people, or to associate myself with them. Shari felt for each and every one, however, and I could see the toll it took on her. She had married me thinking that we might make a peaceful life together. Now she found herself the living symbol of all that can go wrong in even the most ordinary and carefully ordered life. Almost from the beginning, the disarray of my first family had intruded upon our marriage. The emotional upheavals created by the ongoing battle over Dave, the earlier problems with Jeff's alcoholism, and then later with his arrest for child molestation, these had surely been enough to rip at the heart of any marriage. Certainly, such grim complications were not part of what Shari had bargained for in marrying me. But now, in addition to all that, she had been picked up by the tornado of Jeff's crimes, and as the weeks passed, it became clear that she might never be put down by it. Without knowing it, without my having ever given her the slightest hint of it, she had married into a nightmare that might never end.

Day by day, as the months passed, I saw the strain of this new reality eat away at my wife, both physically and mentally. I saw her health deteriorate, her generally buoyant mood darken into a grim resignation. I saw her sleepless, saw her crying, saw her exhausted and depressed. I did not know what to say or do about any of these things. I could see the stain of my first marriage sinking into my second, see Jeff's crimes poisoning everything. A terrible sense of helplessness settled in upon me, and I felt myself become like Jeff, a man who had nothing to offer but a dull, "I'm sorry."

I returned to work for the first time on Tuesday, August 6. A few of my coworkers expressed their sympathy and offered any assistance I might need. Others admitted that they were at a loss as to how they should react or what they should say. Still others went directly to their duties, avoiding the issue altogether. One worker said simply, "There but for the grace of

God, Lionel," by which he meant that it could happen to any father.

Shari returned to her office not long after I did. She confronted a similar situation. Her fellow workers greeted her casually, and then went about their business, pretending as much as possible that nothing whatever had happened. This was understandable, of course. What was there to say?

In general, however, work once again became my refuge, safer than my home, the place to which I could escape from the whirlwind that circled my house, that intruded upon my life with letters I did not want to read, phone calls I did not want to answer, a marriage that at times appeared to be disintegrating.

There were other calls I had to answer, however. One of them was to the duty of being a son. In the weeks following Jeff's arrest, my mother's health had begun to decline rapidly, both mentally and physically. At this time, she was no longer living in the family home, the one she had lived in for fifty-one years. Jeff's crimes, and their subsequent notoriety, had made it impossible for her to remain in the house she and her husband had built in 1939. Consequently, soon after Jeff's arrest, and in order to secure her safety, my mother had been moved to a friend's house. After that, she would never again tend the garden she had worked at for most of her life, and which contained flowers she had brought from her own family's original homestead.

Visiting my mother during her illness was a grueling experience. Suffering now from senile dementia, she had not been able to adjust to her new residence. Each night, she would search for the stairs that had led up to the bedroom of her house in West Allis.

As the months dragged on between Jeff's arrest and trial, I incessantly moved back and forth between the poles of son and father, sometimes even relaying information between my mother and my son. During trips to Milwaukee, I went from my mother's residence to Jeff's prison. On one occasion, I had my mother record a message to my son. Very weak now, her lucidity swimming in and out, my mother labored to record the last message she would ever give to him. Slowly, ponderously, her voice very weak, my mother spoke into the small recorder I placed at her lips. "I love you, Jeff," she said.

On August 28, Shari and I met with Boyle and one of his assistants in order to discuss Jeff's case. This was the first time he had met Shari. We wanted to find out if Boyle was, in fact, going to represent Jeff through the entire court proceeding. If he was, we wanted to know the nature of his defense, and the approximate cost.

The meeting did not go well. It seemed clear to me that Boyle was guarded in answering many of my questions. He claimed that Jeff did not want to see us because he was embarrassed by his crimes. It was better that we not do anything that might increase his stress. In addition, Boyle seemed unable to fix a final fee for his services.

As to Jeff's defense, Boyle said that he was in the process of determining its exact nature. He told me that he was interviewing psychiatrists, psychologists, and forensic experts, and that he would only be able to chart a defense after getting their input.

When I left the meeting, I felt befuddled, unable to understand where I stood in Jeff's defense, if any-where. Perhaps more than at any other time, I felt that my son's fate had slipped out of my hands. I was never to see Jeff alone! Now his future appeared to rest absolutely in the hands of others. My only task was to "appear" to be his father, to wait patiently for his trial, then to occupy my assigned place in the courtroom, as powerless, and in a sense, as utterly faceless, as the male manikin Jeff had once stashed in the dark closet of his bedroom in West Allis.

By the fall of 1991, Shari and I had heard my son described so often as a monster, a ghoul, a demon, that we felt it time to speak out, to let the world know that there had been another Jeff, a little boy who had been like other little boys. In a sense, we wanted to resurrect that boyhood, though in no way to condone what the man had done. In a sense, we also wanted to speak to the victims' families, to make it known that in "supporting" Jeff, we were in no way supporting what he had done, but were as horrified as they were by his crimes.

And so, on September 10, we consented to our first television interview. It appeared on *Inside Edition,* and was conducted by Nancy Glass.

During the interview, I said that I felt a very great responsibility for what my son had done, along with a "deep sense of shame." Then my voice broke suddenly, and I quickly reached for the glass of cola that had been put on the table beside me, and ducked behind it. My words somewhat muffled, I continued, my voice still cracking slightly as I spoke. "When I disassociate myself from this thing," I said, "I'm OK."

"Do you forgive your son?" Ms. Glass asked pointedly.

"That's a tough question," I replied. I paused a moment, then added, "I cannot say that I forgive him."

When I look at that video now, I see a very controlled man, dressed in a blue suit and dark tie, a man hiding behind a glass, a man who will not forgive his son, who powerfully, desperately wants to disassociate himself "from this thing." One can look hard for love in this video, and still not find it. One can find a very great deal of distress. I remember feeling a deep, crushing sense of depression for the victims and for what was ahead for Jeff and us. Watching the video, one can detect a man whose life has been stung by shame, who wants the spotlights to go off so that he can return to the shadows, but it is hard to find a father racked by grief and care. It is "this thing" that he wants to be rid of, "this thing," as I believe now, the horror of what my son had done.

Clearly, it is not a very flattering view of myself, particularly when compared with the sweetness and sincerity of Shari's appearance, the openness of her manner, the obvious care that flowed from her. Still, it was not a vision of myself that I could deny, and I never expected a worse one to be offered.

But a worse one was offered very soon indeed. One that was much worse.

Two days later, on September 12, the Geraldo Rivera show devoted its entire program to Jeff's case. In harrowing detail, Tracy Edwards recounted his escape from Jeff's apartment, and Jeff's later arrest. In his version of events, my son emerged not only as a brutal killer, but as a psychologically sadistic one. According to Edwards, Jeff had threatened and terrorized him, telling him that he intended to eat his heart.

Certain relatives of the victims appeared—heartbroken, as could be expected—and mourned the death of their loved ones. They spoke with dignity about their loss, and with justifiable anger at how Jeff had slipped through the hands of those governmental agencies that should have caught him.

Two other guests shocked and appalled me, however. Pat Snyder, a former Ohio acquaintance, who knew nothing of our family and had met Jeff no more than three times, each time very briefly, accused Shari of being "the epitome of the evil stepmother," which was as deep and hurtful a lie as one human being has ever told about another.

Shari, who had watched the show at her office, was stunned by Snyder's appearance, particularly in light of that fact that she, Snyder, had called me from Charleston, South Carolina, on previous dates, begging to let her write a book about Jeff.

But far worse than anything Pat said was the accusation of a man who refused to give his identity and who sat behind a screen while making the accusation. "Nick" claimed that he had maintained an extended homosexual relationship with Jeff. It had begun at the end of June 1985, and had continued for the next two months. According to "Nick," Jeff had been a jealous lover, but not a violent one, and as the relationship had deepened, Jeff had finally revealed the darkest secret in his life, the fact that his father had "sexually abused him."

Only eleven days later, "Nick," now out from behind a screen, dressed neatly in a white jacket and blue T-shirt but otherwise in full disguise, with fake hair and mustache, repeated his appalling accusation to Phil Donahue, in spite of the fact that I had provided a warning of this Nick-Snyder act to Donahue prior to air time. "Jeff's first sexual experience," he said, "was with his father." Jeff had continued to be sexually abused, "Nick" added, until the age of sixteen.

My son immediately filed a legal affidavit denying that I had ever sexually molested or abused him. He also denied that he had ever met "Nick."

But Jeff's affidavit was of little comfort. It was a charge that could not be disproved, only lived with, along with the doubts it raised in the minds of others, both the world at large, and the people who knew me.

The accusation of child molestation was the one that hit hardest among the people who had known me all my life. At work, I imagined that people with whom I had worked for many years were suddenly overwhelmed with doubts about my character. Suddenly, I was no longer cast in the role of devoted and long-suffering father, but as a dreadful and perverse father, one who had sexually abused his eight-year-old son, a practice which had continued for years.

Suddenly, in my mind, I was the accused, rather than the father of the accused, an agent in my son's crimes, perhaps their ultimate cause. Everywhere, I could sense that change, sense the terrible doubt and suspicion that had gathered around me. Looks and glances that were probably entirely innocent, now looked sinister to me, questioning and accusatory. A kind of paranoia gripped me. I wondered how people could believe such a terrible thing about me, if they believed it. And that was part of my confusion, that I absolutely could not be sure what anyone thought about me anymore. I felt that I had lost my identity as a father, and had assumed another one. And terrible as it was, I had no way of proving that it was all a lie, that "Nick" was an imposter. Even Jeff's denials, which came immediately, could not change the atmosphere that had come to surround me.

It was in that mood of accusation that I waited for Jeff's trial. With my own household reeling under the assault of intrusions from without and a terrible friction from within, I entered a suspended world where nothing at all seemed certain.

As a boy, I had always felt oddly helpless; now I felt beyond the help of anyone. Although in the months to come she would give much more, Shari had already given all that could be expected of her. Because by nature she was far more sensitive than I, she had suffered far more than I had, even from the beginning, and even despite the fact that Jeff was not, at least technically, her son. Still, she had always treated Jeff as her own child, and it was very clear to me that she had sensed a good deal more of his youthful loneliness and isolation than I ever had. In addition, since the murders, she had felt more for the pain of the victims and their families than I had been able to feel.

Still, despite Shari's obvious suffering, I felt that I had no resources of my own to offer her, either emotionally or intellectually. To a degree far deeper than I could have known at the time, and far greater than I had ever expected either to understand or to admit, I was a strangely disassociated man, limited in my ability to respond with feeling to another's feeling, often confused by my own lack of responsiveness, and at times, even baffled by what I vaguely recognized as numb or empty or vaguely wounded spaces in my own nature, spaces that, under certain circumstances, might well have generated acts I was still afraid to face.

Jeff in transition, age fifteen, Bath, Ohio

Jeff, almost seventeen, beginning stages of a broken home, Bath, Ohio

CHAPTER TEN

Jeff's trial began on January 30, 1992. During the two weeks of its proceedings, Shari and I stayed at a hotel on the west side of town, registered under the fictitious name that we still use. My mother's house was empty by then, up for sale, although there was little interest, given what had happened in its basement.

Each day, the motel van would drop us off some distance from the courthouse, and Shari and I would walk the rest of the way. By this means, we could conceal the place where we were staying from the press.

The first day was a revelation, shocking and disturbing, a frenzy of reporters, of crowds, of harsh lights and jutting microphones. At our first appearance on the street, a swarm of reporters would descend upon us, screaming questions: "Have you met with Jeff? What does Jeff say? How do you feel about sitting with the victims' families?" They were not really questions, but opportunities to respond. What they wanted was the sound of our voices to go with a glimpse of our faces, a bit of audio to go with the film.

Mobbed by people and half-dazed by camera lights, we would struggle up the stairs, sheriff's deputies sometimes rushing forward to escort us the rest of the way into the building.

Once inside the courthouse, it became obvious that city and state officials had gone to enormous lengths in order to establish security. Metal detectors had been installed at the entrance of the courtroom, and inside it, dogs sniffed about for bombs. An eight-foot barrier of bullet-proof glass had been built in order to protect Jeff. It divided that part of the courtroom in which the actual trial would take place—the judge's bench, along with the prosecution and defense tables—from the spectators' seats. In addition to this security measure, sheriff's deputies had been positioned all about the room. They stood silently, their eyes scanning the room, their hands sometimes fingering their holstered pistols.

Overall, both the building and courtroom gave the appearance of an armed camp. It still seemed inconceivable to me, strange and unreal, that all of these preparations, so vast and so expensive, had been caused by something my son had done. It was impossible for me to reconcile his passivity and facelessness, the monotone of his speech and the flatness of his personality, with the flurry of activity that surrounded me.

Once in the courtroom, we took our assigned

seats, the last two of the right-hand row, directly fac-
ing the judge's bench. By that time, we had been told
not to attend the trial because of the danger it posed
to our lives. Neither Shari nor I could do that, however, since we felt it important to show Jeff that we
had not abandoned him.

To our immediate left, we could see the families
of the victims as they filled the more than forty seats
that had been assigned to them.

On that first day, we saw nothing but horror, ha-
tred, and disgust on the faces of the fathers, mothers,
sisters, and brothers of the men my son had killed. A
small black woman who'd taken a seat next to us
was abruptly pulled away. No one wanted to come
near us.

Flanked by sheriff's deputies, Jeff came into the
courtroom dressed in a wrinkled brown jacket that
was much too small, that made him look seedy and
unkempt. His hair was ruffled, and he did not appear
clean-shaven. He looked depressed and gave off a
sense of embarrassment, of being deeply and helplessly exposed. Despite the graphic quality of his con-
fession, the long hours he'd already spent with various
psychiatrists, the torturous and damning light he had
shown into the darkest quarters of his life, he still
appeared ashamed in the presence of his father.

Since Jeff had already pled guilty to the various
murder charges that had been brought against him,

the purpose of the trial was to determine whether or not he had been insane when he had committed them. It was never a question of guilt, never a question of Jeff's being released, but only of whether he would be placed in a prison, or in a mental institution.

At the time of the trial, I knew only what had been released to the press. Boyle had not been forthcoming with details. There was much he had not told me. It was the trial that divulged these things, and day after day as it proceeded, I found myself having to absorb acts even more perverse and horrifying than the murders themselves.

"I am duty-bound to bring to your attention every single aspect of Mr. Dahmer's life, of Mr. Dahmer's conduct," Boyle began in his initial statement to the jury.

Every single aspect of my son's life and crimes would, in fact, be presented during the following two weeks. Nothing would be left out, not one grueling detail. Day by day, both the prosecution and the defense would take all those who listened to them through a nightmare world of horrible teenage fantasies, a world which led inevitably to those unspeakable things my son had done, to murder and evisceration and even, toward the end, to cannibalism.

The sheer horror of Jeff's crimes, the nauseating filth in which he had lived in Apartment 213, were, in themselves, stunning to me, unimaginably grotesque and horrifying. One excruciating detail followed another while Shari and I sat, frozen in place, at times unable to believe the things we heard, and yet unable to deny that they were true.

During the whole course of the trial, while I sat in my place, staring straight ahead, I felt that the acts being described were those of someone I could not possibly know, much less someone I had brought into the world. I felt no connection at all to the unspeakable things that were described while cameras whirred and reporters, scores of them, scribbled notes, bringing these same horrible things to the world at large. For me, the acts that the defense and prosecution teams described during the trial remained at a horror-movie distance. My son had lived in a hideous world, but I could not see it as a world that bore any relationship to mine. Instead, it was as if I were being forced to watch a horror film I did not want to watch, from which I could learn nothing, and from which I only wanted to escape.

Because of that remove, I left Jeff's trial at its conclusion with no more insight into my son or myself than I'd had when it had begun. I had attended the trial like an innocent bystander, my mind fixed on the technical aspects of the defense's case, its effort to prove Jeff's insanity. And so, throughout the entire two weeks of the court proceedings, I was able to pigeonhole each individual horror in a neat category of physical or psychological evidence. In that way, I made sure that each item was connected exclusively to Jeff, part of his technical defense, a mere trial exhibit, not a human fact at all, and certainly not part of a larger story that was also mine.

And so, it was only much later that I began to rethink not only my relationship with Jeff, but with the impulses that had overwhelmed him, and with the acts that he had carried out. Only then did I begin to realize that there were some areas of my son's mind—such as a feeling of a lack of control over many things in my life—which I had held within myself for years. Certainly, Jeff had multiplied his tendencies and sexual perversions exponentially well beyond my understanding and of course far beyond my capacity to even entertain. Nonetheless, I could see their distant origins in myself, and slowly, over time, I began to see him truly as my son in far deeper ways than I had previously imagined.

As I began to confront Jeff's childhood imaginings, for example, it became clear to me that they had not always been wholly different from my own. While he was still a teenager, Jeff had been shaken and disturbed by odd thoughts and fantasies, impulses that were abnormal, and to some extent, edged in violence. He had, for example, dreamed repeatedly of murder.

While I had never dreamed of murder, I would often awake with a vague feeling that something seriously bad had happened, usually after an attack by a bully.

From approximately the age of eight, and up until my early twenties, I had periodically been seized by a horrifying sensation of something remembered, but not directly experienced. Later, when I described my upsetting dreams to Dr. Robert Kirkhart (a nationally renowned clinical psychologist), he remarked that he would have been disappointed in me if I had not had any reaction to attacks from bullies. In the grip of that unreal memory, I would wake up suddenly with the frightening sense of foreboding. Once awakened, I would not be able to recall any of the details, but I remained convinced that something bad had happened. Even though I had no vision of a crime, no physical details, no slaughtered bodies, no weapons, no blood-spattered murder rooms, I nonetheless could not shake myself from the feeling of fear and dread. The sensation would last for no more than a minute or so, but during that awful interval, when I would literally hang between fantasy and reality, I would be terrified. I would feel lost, as if everything had gone out of control. Hot flashes would sweep over me with such shattering force that even in adulthood, I would still be able to remember the terror that had seized me at those moments.

As I later both remembered and reconsidered the courtroom description of Jeff's murder of Steven Tuomi, it was this childhood dream, along with its accompanying sense of helplessness and horror, that suddenly returned to me with astonishing clarity and force.

Steven Tuomi was from a small town in Michigan. He was twenty-five years old. On November 27, 1987, he got off from his job as a cook at George Webb's Restaurant. He'd been working there since September, always on the third shift, the one that ended at six in the morning. Across the street, the 219 Club had just closed, and Tuomi strolled over to mingle with the men who'd gathered outside the building. It was there, in front of the club, that he met my son.

A few minutes after the meeting, Jeff and Tuomi went to the Ambassador Hotel. They had continued drinking, then both of them had passed out. That was all Jeff was ever able to remember, other than that when he'd awakened the following morning, he had found himself lying on top of Tuomi's naked body.

According to Jeff's own account, he had eased himself from the body, then, in horror, glanced down and noticed that a trail of blood ran from Tuomi's mouth, that his chest had been beaten in, and that his whole upper body was black and blue.

Clearly, Jeff had beaten him to death.

But Jeff had no memory of it. None at all. He had awakened, as I had awakened at times in my youth, with a strong but vague feeling that something horrible had happened. The big difference was that Jeff had actually done something deeply awful. I had awakened in a panic that consciousness had soon ended. Jeff had awakened into a nightmare that would never end.

Later, after his arrest, after Jeff had admitted not only all the other murders, but the whole, dreadful list of the other things he had done, he would continue to insist that he could recall nothing about the actual murder of Steven Tuomi. He claimed that he had lifted himself up from Tuomi's body and been overcome with shock and horror. Perhaps alone in all the world, I felt I knew exactly what he was talking about, because it had happened to me as well. The only difference, it seemed to me, was that I had awakened out of a nightmare, and my son had awakened into one.

The description of the events surrounding the murder of Steven Hicks called forth other, different, but no less disturbing associations.

Jeff had picked up Hicks on June 18, 1978. He had been driving his mother's car, and had spotted Hicks, who was hitchhiking alongside the road. Hicks had taken off his shirt, so that he was naked to the waist, and it was this that had initially attracted Jeff. He'd pulled the car over, offered Hicks a ride, and then took him to the house on Bath Road.

At the house, Jeff offered beer and marijuana. Hicks accepted both. He had also talked about his girlfriend, something which no doubt ended any hope my son might have had for a homosexual encounter. Sometime later, Hicks tried to leave, and it was then that Jeff had grabbed the steel rod of a barbell from his closet and murdered him.

Later, when I thought over the courtroom recreation of this first of my son's murders, it was clear that it was the prospect of Hick's departure that had sent Jeff over the line.

This dread of people leaving him had been at the root of more than one of Jeff's murders. In general, Jeff had simply wanted to "keep" people permanently, to hold them fixedly within his grasp. He had wanted to make them literally a part of him, a permanent part, utterly inseparable from himself. It was a mania that had begun with fantasies of unmoving bodies and proceeded to his practice of drugging men in bathhouses, then on to murder, and finally, to cannibalism, by which practice Jeff had hoped to ensure that his victims would never leave him, that they would be part of him forever.

In my own life, I realized that I had had the same extreme fear of abandonment, a fear so deep that it generated a great deal of otherwise inexplicable behavior.

It began when I was a very young boy and my mother went into the hospital for an operation. During that time, my aunt and uncle came over to take care of me, but their presence did not relieve what I remember now as a profound sense of isolation and abandonment. My mood darkened, as my mother told me later, and remained in that darkness during all the time of her absence. During all of that extended period, according to my aunt and uncle, whose description was later relayed to my mother, I had cried incessantly and inconsolably, gripped by what could probably be described as a childhood depression that lasted for many weeks.

Shortly after this episode and after my mother returned home, I developed a severe stuttering problem. I can remember stomping my feet on our kitchen floor in an effort to force the words out. My father took me to special classes to overcome this embarrassing affliction. The kids made fun of it in school, but eventually my dear father's dedication and special classes largely ended the stuttering.

I can only imagine how different my life might have been had this morbid fear deepened into pathology. What might I have been, and to what perverse lengths would I have gone, if I had finally developed a psychotic need for things that were fixed in place, without wills of their own, motionless? Would I, too, have at last reduced human beings to "things" that I could "keep"?

Even though I had never reached that extreme, of course, I had, it seemed to me, reached others.

I had relentlessly clung to a first marriage that was deeply wounded. I had clung to routines and habits of thought. To guide my behavior, I had clung to highly defined personal roles. It struck me that I had clung to all these things because they had given me a profound sense of permanence, of something I could "keep." Perhaps I had clung to my roles as father and son for the same reason, because they anchored both my mother and my sons to me, made it impossible for them to drift away. In a sense, I had devoted my life to finding strategies by which I could hold things forever and keep them permanently within my grasp.

Even more to the point, however, was the sense of control that my own need for permanence and stability had generated in me, along with the accompanying dread of anything that I could not control. As I rethought my son's crimes, the themes of permanence and control wove in and out like two dark threads, their intersecting lines forming the net that held everything else together.

In the months after the trial, as I tried to delve into Jeff's mind, I began to look at the psychiatric testimony which had been given at the trial, but this time in a manner that was considerably different from the way I'd listened to it while the trial was still going on. At that time, I had tucked it neatly away, hearing it as technical evidence only, observations that had almost no relationship to my own life. In that way, I had been able to distance myself from what the psychiatric evidence might otherwise mean, both to Jeff and to me.

But once I began to explore my own connections to Jeff, the disturbing implications of the psychiatric testimony emerged for the first time. Soon it became obvious to me that the theme of control had played a part in almost every aspect of Jeff's nature. It was a fact that it had been pointed out repeatedly in court, both by the defense and the prosecution, and yet, at the time I'd heard it, I simply hadn't gotten it. I had filed it under the general category of Jeff's insanity, and left it there, dismissing it as just one more cog in the crazy machinery of his profound mental illness.

But it was more than a cog, as I have come to realize. It was a vital part of the engine that drove him forward, and it was visible in almost everything he did.

Even Jeff's first fantasies involved control. More than anything, he seen himself "laying" with someone who was very still. He had not wanted to be constrained by the people who populated his fantasies. He had not wanted them to press their own sexual needs upon him. Instead, he had wanted to control them absolutely, and had been willing to use violence to gain that control.

For example, on the first occasion when Jeff actually set out to have sexual relations with another person, he carried a baseball bat with him. He had seen a jogger and was attracted to him. He had subsequently lain in wait, hoping the catch the jogger as he passed him, knock him unconscious, and then "lay" with him on the ground.

Still later, when he began to frequent the bathhouses, he had drugged the men he met there, then lay down beside them and listened to their hearts and stomachs, reducing their individual identities to mere parts and functions, to the sounds that came from their bodies after he had made it impossible for them to speak. As his mania for control deepened, it began to function as a necessary element of his sexual satisfaction. So much so, that in the vast majority of cases, he had not been able to reach orgasm unless his partner was unconscious.

But even drugged men finally awakened, and in doing that, began once again to exercise their own individual wills. By then, Jeff had developed such a psychotic need for control that the mere presence of life itself had come to threaten him. So he began to concentrate on the dead. He looked through the obituary columns, found a funeral notice for an eighteen-year-old boy, and plotted to dig up the corpse and bring it home so that he could enjoy that level of control which only could be gotten from the dead.

By then, fantasies of complete control were the only kinds my son had. I now realize that the need for control and permanence, as well as introversion, were traits that I shared with Jeff. Tragically, Jeff took these traits to extraordinary, twisted, and horrific extremes. Jeff hatched a crude scientific scheme for lobotomizing the men he had already drugged, but who, if not lobotomized, would soon return to consciousness, a state Jeff had come to find unacceptable in another human being. So while they were still alive, my son drilled holes in their skulls and poured muriatic acid into their brains. Usually it was an experiment that killed his victims immediately, although one of them survived for a full two days.

Jeff's hope of making "zombies" never worked, but he still had other plans. He still had the dead bodies of his victims, bodies he could deflesh and eviscerate, preserving certain parts and devouring others, but always in order to live out his need for complete control.

Odd as it seems to me now, as I sat in court and listened to all this—the terrible evidence both of my son's insanity and the crimes that had flowed from it—I could see nothing but their grotesqueness and perversity.

One memory in particular returned to me. It concerned a little girl named Junie who lived across the street from me when I was a young boy, around twelve or thirteen. One afternoon I brought her up to my bedroom, lit a candle, sat her in front of it, and began to murmur the "you are getting sleepy" phrases that I had learned from a book and record I'd sent away for some weeks before. They had dealt with hypnotism, and I had sent away for them because, in my own childlike way, I saw its mystifying powers as a means by which I could control people whom I could not otherwise control. It would allow me to turn them into hypnotized zombies, so that I could do whatever I wanted with or to them.

Junie was my first experiment, and when I brought her to my room that day, I intended to cast a spell over her, so that I could control her entirely. With that goal in mind, I told Junie to stare at the candle, and she did so. I told her to close her eyes at the appropriate moment, and she did that, too. I told her to breathe deeply, and she did. I told her to raise her arms over her head. She obeyed instantly. I remember that I felt exhilarated as I watched her, felt truly powerful, truly in command of another human being. Junie was doing everything I asked. She was hypnotized; however, she fell off the chair and woke up.

Later in life, I would often tell this story, but always lightly, as if it were simply a childhood adventure. Thus, even though I was later to make light of the story, it is clear to me now that the act itself betrayed a strong urge to control her.

And so now, when I remember this incident, I can no longer see it as a simple childhood prank, a harmless little boy dabbling in a newfound magic. Instead, I remember the sense of power that came over me as Junie sank into her trance. I remember how much I liked controlling her, and how much I enjoyed, however briefly, that sense of giving commands and having them instantly obeyed. I remember all of this as an event in my psychological history that suggests how much, even as a boy, I had yearned to control other people, how powerless I had often been made to feel in the presence of people I did not control.

When I look back on my childhood, I see its continuing theme as a reaction against my own pervasive sense of powerlessness, that dreadful feeling that I could not do anything right, could not control anything, could not take charge. More often than anything during my childhood, I was plagued by the certainty that I was both physically weak and intellectually inferior.

As a young boy, I was almost the stereotype of the weak, skinny kit, the last to be picked for any sports team. I was the elementary-school kid who was bullied, the kid who was easily frightened, the kid who had glasses and was called "four eyes." In high school, I was the kid the girls hardly noticed, except as an object of curiosity, the kid who never even had a date until he was eighteen, the kid who finally decided that a "great body" was what the girls wanted, and who then methodically went about the task of creating one, working out three times a day until the "skinny kid" had been replaced by someone else.

But if, in the end, I was able to feel less physical inferior, my sense of being intellectually inferior remained very deep and distressing.

My parents were both school teachers, and they carried the value system of school teachers. For them, a good academic performance was to some degree the measure of overall competence.

But I was an average student, slow to learn, particularly in math. From the first grade onward, my parents tried to help me become a better student by drilling me. My father spent countless hours tutoring me. My mother spent almost as much time making flip cards in addition and subtraction, multiplication and division, and by constantly quizzing. The idea that I developed was that I had to "overstudy" everything, and that if I did not, I would fail. Other children might pick things up quickly, but I felt that I was not so fortunate.

Though my mother never intended it, and was only trying to help me, a feeling of personal incompetence overwhelmed me during those early years. It was made more obvious by her extraordinary ability to assert herself, to take charge of things. On one occasion, she berated my Little League baseball coach in front of the whole team for not putting me in to pitch. It was a forceful and commanding personal style that was sometimes demonstrated in Cub Scouts and other activities. Compared to such a force, I naturally saw myself as weak and inept. As a result, of course, I began to develop a feeling of nearly complete powerlessness and dependency.

Even more telling, however, was my mother's tendency to finish things for me before I had a chance to complete them myself. I would start some task, working slowly through it, as I always did, and suddenly my mother would appear, and in a few quick strokes, either of mind or hand, she would finish it for me. Even though done with a helpful, loving intention, such gestures powerfully reinforced my sense of myself as slow and inept and caused me to doubt my ability to do things, to carry through, to complete even the simplest tasks. The net effect was corrosive, leaving me feeling undermined and powerless.

In retrospect, I can see this feeling of being powerless may have led to my adolescent interest in making percussion bombs. My initial interest in making sound explosives was first kindled by my Boy Scout leader, who showed us how to make simple explosive devices with simple ingredients.

While still in high school, I sent away for certain chemicals that were too dangerous to be included in a department store chemistry set. When they arrived, I mixed them into an explosive mixture that could be set off by percussion, that is, by throwing it or dropping it. Then I poured the explosive powder into a homemade cardboard tube with a cardboard bottom. I topped the mixture with BB pellets, which more or less turned it into a sound grenade. On one occasion, a boy riding a bike was so startled by the sound of the explosion he fell off his bicycle. Another time, I gave one to my friend Tom Jungck, who dropped it from the third-floor stairwell of our school, setting off an explosion that was so loud that a group of teachers and the principal gathered in the hallway, holding students back in case the bomb was not spent. They never found out who made or dropped the bomb, but the kids in my school knew who the bomb maker was, and I got a great sense of control and respect from them for being able to create such a powerful device.

Of course, edgy pranks are not uncommon in adolescence, but I now recognize that my interest in making explosives came from a need to assert myself, to feel less threatened. Plagued by feelings of both physical and intellectual inferiority, a bomb afforded me a great sense of control. Although I didn't talk about it much, it gave me a sense of power. It was my way of protecting myself and letting the world know that I was not to be trifled with, that I was not the weak, dull, skinny runt they imagined me to be. To some part of me, the ability to make a bomb made me formidable, and in doing so, it also made me "visible." With the bomb I was no longer a faceless nonentity.

As the years passed, of course, I put my bombs aside. I found other ways of asserting myself and gain-ing a sense of control. I developed other, less dangerous strategies, but at times, even these still seemed to be driven by a sense of desperation, compelled by feelings of inferiority and a frantic need to control every aspect of my life. As a young man, I had become a bodybuilder in order to gain power physically. In college, I relentlessly pursued one degree after another until I finally got my claim to intellectual power, a Ph.D. By those means, I fought my way out of childhood, leaving sound bombs and hypnotism behind me, like forgotten toys.

Under the dark and seemingly inescapable shadow of my son's life, I often reflect on my own childhood. Theoretically, I know we all view the past through the lens of the present, but even knowing that, it is still hard to view my own childhood in an innocent light. Often my childhood memories are locked in a bleak cell, darkened by questions and dread. How close was I to going down a path Jeff went? Was it the difference of choices I did or didn't make, was it due to good or bad genetic luck? I'll never know, but I can't help but wonder if my interest in hypnotization and making explosive devices was something other than a boy's fascination with things unknown. When I wired the couch in our living room to give cousins a little electric shock, was that merely a practical joke? And what about my need for control? Were all these things, and many others, nothing more than normal childhood thoughts and actions, or were some of them early expressions of something dangerous in me, something that might finally have attached itself to my sexuality, and in doing that, turned me into the man my son became?

Final residence—Columbia Correctional Institution, Portage, Wisconsin. Picture taken of Jeff and Lionel during an April 1993 visit, while other inmates and families looked on

CHAPTER ELEVEN

Jeff's trial ended on Friday, February 14, 1992. In his closing statement, Boyle tried once again to show that although Jeff had done terrible things, he had done them in a state of madness. Although he had known what he had done, Boyle argued, he had not been able to control himself. The prosecutor, of course, said otherwise, dismissing the defense's insanity plea as nothing more than a means by which Jeff could escape responsibility for his crimes.

On Saturday, February 15, at a little after four o'clock, Shari and I returned to the courtroom to hear the jury's decision. As count after count was read, the verdict remained the same. They found that Jeff had not suffered from any mental disease, and held him fully responsible for his crimes.

There was a round of cheers from the victims' families, as well as from other people in the courtroom. Shari and I sat silently, our faces very still.

Although tense at first, our relationship with the victims' families had improved during the preceding two weeks. On one occasion, during a break in the proceedings, Mrs. Hughes, Tony Hughes's mother, had approached us, assuring us that she bore us no ill will, that she did not blame us for what Jeff had done. Shari and I had each hugged her and expressed our great sympathy for what had happened to her son. In addition to Mrs. Hughes, a Reverend Gene Champion had also approached us, trying to bridge the gap between us and the victims' families.

But the tension had begun to build again as the trial came to an end, and it only increased as we reached the day Jeff was to be sentenced.

That day was Monday, February 17, 1992, and Jeff arrived dressed in bright-orange prison clothes. He took his seat before the judge and waited for Victim Impact Statements, a procedure that allows crime victims to speak directly to the judge before he passes sentence.

During the next few minutes, as Shari and I looked on, several members of the victims' families spoke about what my son had done to them. Mrs. Hughes, the mother of Tony Hughes, was very dignified. She spoke of her son, then made the American Sign Language symbol for *I love you.* Other family members were equally dignified. They talked about their loss, about how much they loved and missed the son or brother my son had taken from them. They were emotional, as they had a right to be, but they remained carefully controlled. Only

Rita Isabel, the sister of Errol Lindsey, lost control. Shouting obscenities, she actually stepped from behind the podium and rushed at Jeff. Court officials restrained her, and after that, the judge refused to allow any more statements.

Then Jeff spoke, his voice very quiet. "I am so very sorry," he said.

After the decision, Jeff was rushed directly back to the library adjacent to the judge's chambers. We were allowed to see him for only a few minutes. He was very shaken, trembling, nearly in tears. He was clearly shocked that he had been sentenced to prison, rather than a mental institution.

We had ten minutes to say good-bye to Jeff. For the first time, I saw him frightened about being sent to prison, rather than a mental facility. We held him, told him we loved him, and I said a prayer for us all. Then we waited in another room while the courtroom was cleared and it was safe for us to leave the building. While there, a sheriff's deputy handed me a clear plastic bag that contained Jeff's clothes.

We exited through a maze of corridors and staircases until we were finally escorted through the kitchen and out into the unmarked sheriff's car that whisked us away from the press frenzy. The speed at which it had all come to an end was blinding, perhaps even a bit anticlimactic. Within an instant, it was over. A quick good-bye, and my son was gone.

At the end of Jeff's trial, conviction, and sentencing, I suppose Shari and I expected our lives to return to something that at least resembled normalcy. We gave what we fully expected to be our final interview on the case, the two of us once again speaking on *Inside Edition*. During the interview, Shari wept for the suffering of the victims' families. I expressed my sorrow as well, but then went on to suggest that my son's madness might well have been caused by the prescribed medications Joyce had taken during her pregnancy. (While it is true, of course, that the medications may not have contributed anything to Jeff's equation, it is also true that no one at any time addressed the issue of possible genetic changes during conception and the early stages of pregnancy.) Clearly, at that time, any deeper consideration of the relationship I had with Jeff, either emotionally or biologically, still remained beyond my grasp.

In the meantime, Jeff had been sent to Columbia Correctional Institution, a full eleven-hour drive from our home outside Akron. Little by little, as the weeks passed, there were fewer articles in the press, fewer episodes in the news. I went back to my job, and Shari went back to hers. We still received crank phone calls from time to time, and we still receive kind, sympathetic letters.

As a father, it was both my duty and my desire to keep in touch with Jeff, despite the distance, to help him in any way I could. I also felt it my duty to change his legal counsel. Consequently, Robert and Joyce Mozenter were hired to represent Jeff in his upcoming hearing in Akron, the one during which he intended to plead guilty to the murder of Steven Hicks, a murder which had occurred in Ohio, and for which he could not be tried in Wisconsin.

I did not see that there was much more that I could do for Jeff. He was now totally in the hands of other people. They would decide what he wore, what he ate, where he slept, what medication, if any, he received. My fatherly duties had been reduced to the provision of a few small services, none of them basic. As a father, my role had almost disappeared.

But as a son, it was becoming more arduous. Shortly after Jeff's trial, it became obvious that my mother could not continue to live in her apartment, even with the custodial care that had been provided for her. From visit to visit, it was clear that she was failing rapidly. At night, she was rarely lucid, and it had become increasingly difficult to keep her in bed, or to maintain any form of conversation. Even more trying was the fact that she absolutely could not accept the apartment as her home. It was a strange place to her, and she could not adapt to it. Even so, there was no question but that she could not return to the house in West Allis.

And so, it became necessary to find another place for my mother to live. We found one a few weeks later, and on March 29, Shari and I went to gather my mother's things from the apartment she had lived in since Jeff's arrest. "It was a sad gathering," as I wrote later to Jeff, then adopted my usual tone of fatherly guidance. I told him to take his medication dutifully, to use his mind "to a sense of satisfaction," and to "stay well mentally," with "God's intervention and control."

"You are loved greatly by me!" I wrote at the end of the letter, allowing the single explanation point to carry the weight of my emotions.

During the next few weeks, I wrote to Jeff often. In a letter written on April 3, I offered yet more practical advice. I told Jeff that I hoped that he would "get increasingly better with respect to feeling resigned to your situation." At the same time, I added that he should "resolve to accomplish some goals that you will decide." I told him that I knew it must be hard for him to adjust to prison, but that I recognized that life outside of it must have been a torment, too.

*   *   *

A few weeks after Jeff had been transferred to Columbia Correctional Institution, Boyle faxed a letter telling me that Jeff was back in segregation for having secreted a razor blade in his cell. It had been discovered in a routine check of his personal property, and it was the type used in plastic disposable razors.

In response, I called CCI and spoke with Jeff's prison psychiatrist. He assured me that the prison took Jeff's attempt to steal a razor blade very seriously, and that he had been placed on suicide watch. In addition, he said, Jeff had been put on Prozac, a potent antidepressant which he thought would be able to lift Jeff out of his severe depression. This would not happen immediately, he added, since it would take a couple of weeks for the drug to build up in his system.

A short time later, Shari and I drove first to Milwaukee, then the additional two-hour drive to Columbia Correctional Institution.

When Jeff was brought into the visiting room, he appeared haggard and depressed, his hair disheveled, his face unshaven. He looked as if he had not slept for a long time.

After the usual greetings, I asked about the razor.

"I took it in case it got too bad in the future," Jeff told me.

I tried to be encouraging, to help him make the

best he could of his life. He responded as he always had, nodded quietly, agreeing with everything I said but offering very little in return. After that, we talked about my mother's condition, what he'd been eating, the condition of our cats.

On our way out, prison authorities gave us a box of items which had been sent to Jeff, along with a vast amount of mail. As we drove home that evening, Shari began reading the letters to me as she sat in the passenger seat, one hand holding the flashlight she needed to see the writing clearly.

The variety was astonishing, letters that began with such salutations as "Greetings in the Name of the Great I Am," or simply, "Hello, It's Me Again," and ending with everything from "Sincerely a Servant of the King of Kings" to "Lonesomely Yours."

Predictably, a great many were religious, written by people who were attempting to save Jeff's soul, and who often included religious literature of one kind or another, usually pamphlets small enough to be tucked into a regular letter envelope. A few notes were from teenagers seeking prison pen pals. Still fewer were frankly sexual, some from men, some from women, but all of them filled with descriptions far too explicit to be mentioned here.

There were love letters, as well. One woman wrote to tell Jeff that she'd bleached her jeans and emblazoned his initials on them. "We are destined to

be together," another woman wrote. In still other letters, Jeff was addressed as "babe, doll, darling, my
lovely." One woman described him as "cute and
keen."

Other people wrote Jeff in less romantic terms.
"You seem like a very intelligent person to me," one
man wrote. "I mean, you was making nine dollars an
hour."

Some letters came from autograph seekers and
souvenir hunters. Many requested that Jeff meet with
them in prison. One woman asked only that he agree
to meet with her in Heaven.

Other letters kept Jeff up-to-date on the latest "Jeffrey Dahmer" jokes. One woman sent him all the
lyrics to "You've Got a Friend."

Still fewer came from people who were deeply
disturbed themselves. Of these, some were relatively
mild. "My dream told me that your mental illness was
complex, but explainable," one man wrote, "just like
mine was." Another was more chilling: "The doctors
at this institution underestimate what I am capable
of!" Still others suggested an even deeper derange-
ment: "I'm sure the mutilation of my first sucker will
be very crudely done." Racists sent my son their heartfelt congratulations for having murdered so many
young black men. One wanted to know whether he'd
picked up his ideas while stationed in Germany.

In a sense, letters such as these were dismissible.

They spoke to a small and deeply troubled segment of the population. There were others, however, that seemed to embrace a larger group, the whole vast sadness of the world. "I know what it's like to be lonely," one woman wrote. "My husband was my whole world, and when he died, I wanted to go with him." Letter after letter formed a long chain of immemorial complaint: "My fiancé is an alcoholic." "I've just broken up with my boyfriend." "I get dizzy spells." "I am on Dilantin for my epilepsy." "I have this problem with my husband." "I wish I could go back to my high-school years." "I never went to college." "I have trouble learning how to back the van up at work." "I can't express myself on paper." "I get pissed off all the time." "My plant just had another layoff." "No one likes my music." "No one understands me." "No one cares." "Sometimes all I feel is hate."

Some of these letters clearly deepened into grave emotional distress: "When I go to sleep, I die," wrote one woman. "I feel so miserable, I just don't care," said another. To these were added dozens of other similar complaints: "I can't sleep anymore"; "I am always shaking"; "I feel so lost"; "I feel numb"; "I seem so negative all the time"; "I am so limited."

Clearly, some of these people believed that in some bizarre way, my son could rescue them from lives in which they felt entrapped. "Only you can calm me down," one woman wrote. Occasionally, there was even the hint that a connection to my son would make a sinister solution possible. "After I see you," a woman wrote, "the Institution will deal with my husband."

As letters, they came by the hundreds, some with envelopes bearing drawings of animals, religious scenes, or scriptures, some merely bearing quiet pleas for a miraculous assistance. "SOS Help me!" one said. Another delicately warned: "Small hearts enclosed."

As we drove through the night, Shari would often break down as she read these letters, the flashlight trembling in her hand, tears rolling down her cheeks. It was a response that baffled me in its intensity and passion, in the way it demonstrated a level of sympathy and pity that I simply could not reach. Watching her, I often wondered why, in a world of so much feeling, I could express so little.

On May 1, 1992, Jeff appeared in criminal court in Akron, Ohio, and pleaded guilty to the murder of Steven Hicks. He was flown down from the Columbia Correctional Institution, arriving somewhat early, and through the auspices of Sheriff Troutman and the Summit County Sheriff's Department, Shari and I were able to visit with him for a short time on the night before the scheduled hearing.

We met Jeff at the Summit County Sheriff's Department. He looked much better than usual. And although he was dressed in casual prison clothes, he looked very neat and clean. He was nervous, as he was so often nervous, but he was not entirely withdrawn. For about half an hour, we talked about things peripherally related to the hearing, and I assured him that he would only be in court for an hour or so, and that there was no need for him to be nervous. The proceedings, I told him, were cut-and-dried. There would be no surprises of any kind.

The next day, only a few minutes before the hearing, Shari and I met with Jeff again. At this meeting, Jeff was clearly apprehensive about the scheduled hearing. He feared the same kind of media assault he'd faced in Milwaukee, but in addition, he dreaded the prospect of confronting the parents of Steven Hicks, or of hearing, once again, the details of their son's murder. We said a brief prayer as we all held hands.

"It'll be all right, Jeff," I assured him.

He did not look so sure.

"It's just a formal thing," I added, "something that you have to do."

Jeff nodded softly, as resigned as ever.

I smiled. "You look good, Jeff," I said.

Which was true. He was dressed in a clean suit and neat dress shirt, but had not yet put on his tie.

"You should do your tie now," I told him. "We'll probably be going into the courtroom soon."

Jeff looked at me helplessly.

"Go ahead," I said, "tie your tie."

Jeff didn't move. "I can't," he said.

"Why not?"

He shrugged. "I don't remember how," he said.

And so I stepped up to him, wrapped the tie around his neck, knotted it, and drew it neatly up against his throat.

"Now it looks good," I said.

Jeff smiled slightly. "Thanks, Dad," he said.

Within moments, he was led into the courtroom. The hearing lasted little more than an hour. The Mozenters were there as Jeff's lawyers, and Larry Vuillemin appeared as local counsel on Jeff's behalf. Overall, the proceeding was handled with great dignity. There were no legal pyrotechnics, no press frenzy. At the end of it, Jeff was sentenced to life imprisonment without possibility of parole.

Once the hearing was over, Jeff was quickly taken back to the waiting room, where we were given five minutes to say good-bye. He was still wearing the tie I had knotted for him.

*   *   *

A few weeks later, on June 9, 1992, I assured Jeff that I would soon be able to pick up those of his personal possessions which the police had seized from his apartment in Milwaukee.

Then, predictably, I launched into a numbing discussion of my work. "I just got finished analyzing some epoxy compounds at the lab," I wrote. "You have probably used or heard of epoxy cement at some time. These samples contain the epoxy group $C \overset{O}{\diagup \diagdown} C$ and the researchers who submitted these samples to me want to know the percentage of this group in the samples."

Now, when I look at these passages from my correspondence with Jeff, I see them as the perfect representatives of that part of my fatherhood which had always remained intransigently evasive and uninsightful. In its concentration on the trivial minutiae of life, in its emphasis and lack of meaning, in the way it substitutes details for substance, information for feeling, it exhibited my continued determination to evade the disturbing core of both myself and my son, along with the line that indisputably connected us.

In another letter, this one written on July 2, the same characteristics are equally apparent.

In this case, my evasion takes the form of an irrelevant weather report: "I am sitting in my office. It is hot and humid outside. The grass is turning brown due to the lack of rain around here. I have a small fan mounted beside my desk, sitting on top of the cold air register blowing toward me." And so on, and so on, and so on.

The utter emptiness of such lines, their meaningless asides, make the numbing quality of my relationship with him very clear to me. I remember how, years before, after I'd discovered Jeff living alone and more or less abandoned in the Bath Road house, I had essentially turned him over to Shari while frantically searching for my other son, making call after call in a desperate attempt to locate Dave, while all the time Jeff remained only a few miles away, easily within my physical reach, yet far more lost than Dave, far more deprived, and in the deepest sense, as I have come to understand, far more like me than I could have then imagined.

Toward the middle of August, Shari and I visited Jeff at Columbia Correctional Institution. By that time, he had been on Prozac for several months, and his mood had brightened considerably. Although not yet in general population, he was no longer entirely segregated. He was far more animated in his conversation, far more engaged. He talked about the possibility of getting a job in the prison. He mentioned several potential jobs, and seemed to be most interested in those related to the prison's printing shop. An anonymous benefactor had contributed one hundred-thirty dollars to his prison account, and with that money, he had ordered thirteen books, all of them having to do with the creation-evolution controversy. It amazed him that a scientific theory that had been received as an unarguable scientific fact during all the years of his education might rest on questionable assumptions. It seemed to delight him that so thoroughly accepted an idea could be questioned, that nothing stood on truly solid ground.

Shari and I left the prison later that morning, and a few hours after that, in order to relax, we stopped at the Wisconsin State Fair in West Allis. It was a bright, sunny day, and as Shari and I walked the fairgrounds, we could sense that there might be a light at the end of the tunnel when it came to Jeff. He had looked to be in quite good shape, both physically and mentally. We could at least hope that he was learning to adjust to prison life, and that he was going to make the best of it. Given all that, it seemed possible that for a precious few minutes, we might be able to enjoy the casual atmosphere of the fair.

At one point, we stopped to have a late lunch. I stepped up to a booth and bought two Italian sausages and lemonade. There was a dense crowd and we both found something comforting in the openness of the situation, its sea of faces, ours like all the others, pleasant, contented, thoroughly anonymous.

Then, suddenly, as we were making our way toward a table where we could sit together and have our lunch, a blond woman reached out and grabbed Shari's arm.

"Come sit with us," she said. "I know who *you* are."

In September, I received an official list of all the things that had been collected from Jeff's apartment. Sixty-nine separate sheets, all of them headed POLICE INVENTORY, listed the residue of my son's life.

There were the videos he had watched, some innocuous, like *Blade Runner* and *Star Wars,* some darkly suggestive, like *Hellbound* and *Exorcist III,* and still others that were grimly pornographic, *Hardmen II, Rock Hard,* and *Tropical Heat Wave.*

There were the things he had read, all of it pornographic, with the exception of four books on the care of fish.

There was the music he had listened to, Motley Crue and Def Leppard's "Hysteria."

There were the food supplements that had strengthened him: Yerba Prima, Vita, and Anabolic Fuel, incongruously assembled with the junk food of a careless life, Doritos and Ruffles chips.

There were the things that had helped destroy him: bottles of rum and cans of beer, an alcoholic's indiscriminate collection, Budweiser, Pabst Blue Ribbon, Miller High Life.

There were chemicals he had used to clean: Clorox bleach, Woolworth Pine Cleaner, and Lysol. There were chemicals he had used to preserve: formaldehyde and acetone. And there were chemicals he had used to kill: chloroform and ether and halcion, as well as to break down the flesh of the newly dead, Soilex, six boxes. There were even chemicals he had used to conceal the things that he had done: Odor-sorb, also six boxes.

There were utterly neutral things, suddenly made sinister: three black-handled forks, two butcher knives, a pair of chemical-resistant gloves, a handsaw with five detachable blades, and a three-quarter-inch drill.

There were ordinary things, suddenly made unspeakably perverse: barbecue sauce and meat tenderizer.

There were the few things he used to beautify his life: an ornamental driftwood, artificial peacock feathers, and a lighted fish tank.

There were symbols of the modern world: a computer and a software manual, a guide to learning DOS, a blue-and-white laptop box cover. And there were artifacts from an ancient world: two plastic griffins and an incense burner.

There were the things he had used to sustain life: a box of fish food. And the things he'd used to take it: a pair of nickel-plated handcuffs.

There were, at last, the inescapable remnants of the awesome damage he had done, each item grimly listed in the same terrible inventory:

1 Pillow White w/Light Blue Flowers w/Blood Stain
1 Pillow Black Case & Pillow w/Blood Stain
1 Bed Sheet Black Fitted w/Blood Stain
1 White Mattress Cover White w/Blood Stain
1 Pillow Case Black w/Blood Stain
1 Mattress w/Blue Flowered Pattern w/Blood Stains Both Sides

On Saturday, November 28, I went to gather up those things which the police had seized from Jeff's apartment after his arrest and which were in no way related to his crimes. There was quite a lot, so I took a van down to the Safety Building, adjacent to the Milwaukee Police Headquarters.

The police garage was in the basement, and so I drove the van under the building, then backed it up to the warehouse, where Jeff's things had been kept since July of the previous year.

Escorted by three detectives, I walked into a large, concrete storage area. Other men were already assembling Jeff's things at the front of the room. There was more of it than I had expected, and so, for a long time, I watched as they lugged out the larger items:

his television, two black lamps, various tables and chairs—the props used in a life that had been lived on the margin. Never had Jeff seemed more lost than in the things he had possessed.

In December 1992, another innocent victim, my mother, died in the final residence where I had placed her several months before. She died in her sleep, at peace. Shari and I drove up to Milwaukee to make arrangements for her funeral. Two days later, my mother was buried.

After the funeral, we drove up to see Jeff. We had called before leaving our house, and so he already knew of his grandmother's death when we arrived. The night of her death, he told me, he'd experienced a sudden rush of nervousness and dread. "I don't know," he said, "I just felt wired that night, like my nervous system was going to explode." Several hours later, he added, that feeling was gone.

On the way back from Columbia Correctional Institution, with Shari riding beside me, I felt an odd sense of finality. One of the great roles of my life, that of a dutiful son, was over. I was now a father, only.

Once at home, I went to the trunk of the car,

opened it, and picked up the box I'd brought back from Columbia. I took it into the basement, drew back the lids and glanced inside. There was nothing of note, nothing of any particular significance, only the usual items that strangers sent to Jeff for reasons I will never know: canned or packaged food; clothes and vitamins; pencils, pens, and writing pads; crucifixes and rosaries of all kinds; audiotapes; stuffed animals; stamped envelopes, some already self-addressed, others not; books, both hardback and paperback, but usually religious; news magazines; nature magazines; religious magazines; a smattering of *Reader's Digest,* and, of course, hundreds of letters, scores bearing foreign stamps.

For a moment, all these things, gathered together in that small brown box, seemed terribly sad to me, a pathetic and hopeless reaching out in impossible gestures of sympathy and consolation. I had brought all of it back home, and as I began to take these things one by one from the box, I remembered all the other times that I had gone to wherever it was Jeff had lived, gathered up his things, and brought them home. When he'd failed at college, I had brought back his things. When he'd been sentenced for child molestation, I had returned to my mother's house and brought back his things. And at the end of his trial, long after he'd been locked away, I'd driven into the basement of the Safety Building and once again gathered up his things. Now, each month, I returned to him, talked a while, then gathered up his things and brought them home. Nothing, it seemed to me, could better serve as the metaphor for those who live their lives under the shadow of a troubled child than this exhausted, but unending sense of cleaning up.

But what could I have cleaned up of my own? What could I have gathered up and put away so that Jeff might not have gotten to it? In the early years, we pick up everything that would be dangerous for our children to have. We pick up marbles and staples and thumbtacks so that they cannot find and swallow them. We put away knives and guns and poisons and even plastic bags. We plug up electrical outlets and place small pads over all the sharp edges we can find.

But there are other things we cannot protect our children from, and I have come to believe that among these many other things, a few have the potential for a profound and awesome evil. As a scientist, I further wonder if this potential for great evil also resides deep in the blood that some of us fathers and mothers may pass on to our children at birth. In addition to whatever my genetic contribution was, the violence and crime in our society and in the media had a great influence on my son, as well as on the countless other children who are exposed to the glorification of violence that they watch in movies and television. I also believe that a wise, skilled, and loving psychologist might have guided Jeff in his early, formative years into a different ending.

If we are fortunate, we pass our gifts, not only spiritual, intellectual, and physical gifts, but our gift for love and sympathy, our gift for enduring misfortune, for sustaining life, and for honoring it.

But some of us are doomed to pass a curse instead.

When I think back on the interview I gave to *Inside Edition* so many months ago, I hear the interviewer's question once again: "Do you forgive your son?"

Yes, I do.

But should he forgive me?

I am not so sure, because I have come to believe that some of the compulsions that overwhelmed my son may have had their origins in me, and the things I might have done or not done with him. Perhaps it was only by the grace of God that I or any escaped his fate, or because of either genetic endowment or the psychological legacy of my parents and their parents. The odd fantasies of my youth, the violent impulses that arose in me from my early feelings of powerlessness and inferiority, that perhaps limited my expressing my love to Jeff—all these, I believe, may have come to Jeff through me.

For me, the terrible implications of these many possibilities are very deep and painful. And yet, after all that has happened to my son, after all the sorrow and devastation that his life has brought to others, I cannot avoid considering even the darkest of them.

And yet, in the absence of a professional study, I cannot be sure. Although, as a scientist, I must accept genetics as a powerful contributing force in the formation of a human being, I also understand that only half of my son's genetic make-up came from me, and even more, that genetic mutations can occur at any time in any living organism, their influence on later development entirely unpredictable. I don't know, and will never know, how much drugs contributed to Jeff's crimes, either his own alcoholism, or the medications my wife took while he still lay in her womb. Nor can I gauge with any reliability the effect of our disordered family relations during the time that he was growing up, or guess at how therapeutic intervention might have helped him at any given point in his journey toward destruction. Could Jeff have been influenced by the level of violence in our society that surrounded him or by the constant violence that his peer group watched in movies and television?

Now, many months after Jeff's trial and our ordeal, I remain a man in constant rumination, often tortured in soul by the deeds of my offspring. I find that I remain in the grip of a great unknowing, both in terms of Jeff himself, and my effect upon him as a father, by omissions and commissions. Fatherhood remains, at last, a grave enigma, and when I contemplate that my other son may one day be a father, I can only say to him, as I must to every father after me, "Take care, take care, take care."

.

Afterword

Shortly after I arrived at work on November 28, 1994, Shari called to tell me Jeff was dead. A flush swept over me. It was somewhat like the shock I felt, sitting at the same desk in July 1991, when she told me that Jeff had been arrested for murder. Yet it was also a different feeling. I felt as if a part of my innermost being had left me. I was in utter despair.

In a sense, Jeff's murder was the culmination of the swirl of events and emotions which have kept us off balance, wondering What's next? Many things are still happening, however, which continue to cause enormous stress in our lives. My thoughts focus on my loving wife, Shari, who has suffered so much from these pressures. It seems unfair that one who has done so much to promote the strong and caring three-way bond between Shari, Jeff, and me should have to be the one to suffer the most.

Recently, two weeks before her eye surgery, Shari was forced to undergo a long, grueling, court-ordered video deposition in connection with a lawsuit claiming that we "knew or should have known that defendant Jeffrey Dahmer was deviant and destined to cause severe injury and death to others." We were at a loss to explain why Shari was even named as a defendant since she had met Jeff briefly, only once in the spring of 1978. Although several attorneys told Shari they felt she would be quickly dismissed, this lawsuit continued for two years, causing Shari to suffer loss of her work and a worsening of her health problems. Numerous medical and psychological treatments were necessary, and she felt defamed. She had to retain an attorney. Shari puts up a gallant front, but I see her fragility in private. I have wondered to myself, How ironic; Jeff's biological mother wasn't even deposed. We are left with a puzzled and hurt sense of this judicial process, knowing only one thing for certain: Shari didn't deserve to suffer like this.

In contrast, our experiences with people like Theresa Smith have softened the hurting. After our memorial service for Jeff, she said, "I forgive Jeff, Lionel," referring to her dear brother Eddie. I felt surprise and relief as we hugged for what seemed a long time. Shari smiled knowingly as she squeezed my hand and kissed me. Now that Jeff was dead, it was time to focus my life on the people precious to me— Shari first and foremost—and my other son, Dave. These people, and many others, have gone out of their way to console us and share our grief.

People who had shared letters with Jeff have been

contacting us. They said they were shocked and saddened to lose a real friend. There was something naive and different about Jeff, many said. Two people from Adelaide, Australia, wrote, "The media commented that only Jeffrey's family would shed tears. They were wrong." A close friend of mine, a fine parent, gave his deep-felt condolences and said that *A Father's Story* caused him to deeply reflect on his own parenting, and he was going to urge his grown sons to study the book. Comments such as these indicate to me the book is accomplishing one of its intended goals: to help people.

An interviewer asked me about my thoughts on my role in "genetic inheritance," and I realized that there were also some things not made clear in my book. I rolled many thoughts through my mind as I tried to fathom Jeff—genetic influence, environmental influence, etc. My psychologist had warned me, "Lionel, some of the possible influences you have come up with may not be involved at all and, furthermore, I would be disappointed in your intellect level if you suggested that any one of them is solely responsible for Jeff's actions." The point is that I was merely brainstorming in lieu of a scientific study of both genetic and other sources leading to Jeff. In fact, there is no antisocial history in my lineage.

Some may question why I grieve for someone who did what he did. Beyond the usual true responses that he was my son and I have all the loving memories of his very young days, I particularly grieve because for almost a year before he was murdered he had become someone who could have nothing in common with the person who committed the previous terrible acts. His humanity was restoring itself. Shari and I noticed a significant reaching out. During a visit graciously approved by Warden Endicott, Jeff apologized personally to Theresa for the hurt caused her and attempted to answer her need to know that Eddie had not suffered. The Madison, Wisconsin, Church of Christ Minister Roy Ratcliff, who baptized Jeff into Christ and studied with him, responded to someone's statement that the redemption of Jeff stretched his concept of God's grace. Mr. Ratcliff replied that this was really just a simple application of God's grace. He went on to say that the negative part of Jeff's life illustrates how low one can sink when God is not a part of your life and, on the positive side, how high one can rise when God is allowed to take charge of your life. All this was Mr. Ratcliff's way of gently saying that if Jeff's being saved stretches your concept of grace then that concept is smaller than the one described in the inspired scriptures.

A letter written to Mary Mott of Arlington, Virginia, in April 1994 characterizes Jeff's sincerity:

Dear Mrs. Mott,
Hello, thank you so much for sending me the World Bible Correspondence course. Also,

thank you for the Bible! I want to accept the Lord's salvation, but I don't know if the prison will allow me to be baptized. Mr. Burkum, our Chaplain, is not sure if he can find someone that would be able to baptize me in prison; I'm very concerned about this. I hope that this letter finds you well and in good health. God bless you!

Sincerely, Jeff Dahmer

Thus began a series of written contacts between Jeff and several wonderful people besides Mary, ending in the event that Jeff referred to in his letter to Mr. Garland Elkins of Memphis, Tennessee, part of which said: "Yes, I was baptized into Christ on May 10th around 2 pm. It was kind of a strange day to be baptized, because that was the day of the solar eclipse. Around 12 noon, most of the sun was covered, but by 2 PM the sun was bright and shining again. . . . I would like to share the full plan of salvation with other inmates . . ."

In retrospect, it seems that a long line of orchestrated events brought Jeff to this point. In 1989, I myself "returned" fully to God, being influenced by the urging of my son, Dave, and profoundly affected by a seminar presented by a scientist from Montgomery, Alabama, Dr. Bert Thompson. Then, in quick succession, I made contact with a network of scientists from California to Russia. I shared tapes and articles with Jeff up to the time of his arrest in July 1991, and then afterward until his death. Jeff was in the firm grip of his obsessive, compulsive urges, however; nothing got through to him until his final arrest, he said. After his arrest, Jeff said it was like a veil being lifted from him, and he seemed to be able to discuss his ultimate fate and even some of the "discoveries" that I had made and wanted to share with him.

At one visit, Jeff confessed to me that, previously, he did not really feel accountable for his actions, partly because of the things taught in high school and afterward, everywhere he turned. As Jeff explained to Stone Phillips in the NBC "Dateline" interview, when asked his thoughts when he was committing such crimes, "I felt that I didn't have to be accountable to anyone—since man came from slime, he was accountable to no one." While it is, of course, not true that every criminal, or even the ordinary law-abiding person, does wrong because of the hypothesis that we all came from slime, Jeff and I concurred that teaching of only this belief, as fact, has stifled free thinking and affected millions of lives. Jeff had read thirteen books on the origins question, and I truly looked forward to discussions with him. We talked about the latest developments. I told him about the work of a Russian microbiologist friend who was researching the genetic changes in animals. Jeff sounded intrigued when I told him that this work may show why we see changes, but only within apparently prescribed limits. Then, Jeff would respond by saying that even the famous evolutionist Stephen J. Gould of Harvard admits that incontrovertible intermediate forms are nonexistent and that there are seemingly discrete boundaries to gross change. Next, either Jeff or I would say something like maybe the DNA informational programming on a fantastically micro scale is the evidence, right under our noses, showing design by intelligent life out there that Carl Sagan is looking for with his radio telescopes.

It felt stimulating and I miss Jeff's inquiring mind. Some of my friends, relatives, and even family members have accepted the prevailing philosophic belief, without question, concerning our origins. Jeff and I have been fortunate to "hear the other side of the story" and to have shared for a brief time the scientific evidences of intelligent design. Jeff, especially, understood that what we believe about our origins determines what we believe about our destiny. Although we also talked nonstop about personal things, happy and sad, I mention these conversations above to characterize the intensely connected feelings I developed in talking about these subjects with Jeff. He seemed to feel the same way. If only we had somehow made contact with a Bert Thompson fifteen to twenty-five years earlier!

And so, this shared interest, along with the evidence that the change in him seemed sincere, makes it very hard for me emotionally. I find myself sometimes slipping into a morose state, longing for him. I try to divert my mind by throwing myself into my work. Putting my afterthoughts to print is also cathartic, much in the way it was when I had my thoughts put in book form for *A Father's Story*. It is extremely difficult for me, however, as I frequently visualize his badly battered head and body on the cart at the Veteran's Memorial Hospital in Madison, Wisconsin. My pain must be like that of family members of Jeff's victims. In her characteristically reassuring manner, Shari tells me that Jeff is at peace now. Part of me agrees but another part of me wants Jeff to have lived to fulfill his stated desire to share his knowledge and hopes with others. Because Jeff found new direction and goals, he lost his earlier belief that he should be dead for what he did. He did not "have a death wish, with no gumption to kill himself," as some were quoted to say. These people were simply out of touch with Jeff for over two years.

Brian Masters, a well-known British author and thoughtful friend to Shari and me, has been the singular writer having a deep insight into Jeff and the surrounding events. In a recent feature article entitled "But He Did Not Deserve to Die," Brian, like me, asks the question: Why wouldn't it be possible for Jeff to have contributed something worthwhile? Brian cited the notorious Nathan Leopold, who helped discover a cure for malaria and wrote a math textbook while in prison.

Someone said that Jeff was like a "comet which comes around only once in a long time." While it sounds like a good analogy, this misses one of the main points inherent in *A Father's Story*—that is, what Jeff did was the culmination of a long series of progressive involvements with pornography and other obsessions. We are all part of a continuum and, since the consequence of lust is more lust, it is important that parents be especially watchful for developing patterns of obsession in their children (and in themselves). Whether the "lust" manifests itself as sex, power, control, dominance, money, food, or something else, it could in the extreme lead to another Jeff, or in the less extreme to a person anywhere along the continuum of human wrongdoing. In a very human sense, many people may be reluctant to deal with that. They want to say that a little bit of lust is no problem, a little sin is no problem, and it's easier to dismiss Jeff that way, as a rarity having no relevance to them or their children, much like a comet that makes a rare appearance.

Some of the reactions to Jeff's murder were predictable. Congressman Traficant of Ohio ranted to his colleagues something to the effect that we should let all of them just kill each other. A Chicago WLS-AM radio talk-show host proclaimed the day as a celebration and said, "I'm sure if there is a hell, there's a place of special honor there for Jeffrey Dahmer, now." A family member of one of Jeff's victims appeared on a national TV talk show proposing that Jeff's murderer receive a medal. Reports out of Milwaukee had some people considering Jeff's murder to be poetic justice.

Rather than Jeff's murder being any kind of justice, it is just another example of the failure of the criminal justice system. The only message that one gets from the murder of Jeff is "Watch your back in prison!" There is no message of right or wrong. There is only a message of more murder, more hate, more craziness, and more sin. Rather than glorying in Jeff's murder, I believe anyone who is really thinking should feel humiliated that this can be allowed to happen in a super maximum security prison like Wisconsin's Columbia Correctional Institution (CCI).

During one of my visits, shortly after Jeff had been attacked with a razor in July 1994, the prison chaplain was waiting for me in the lobby. After he talked to me, I felt reassured that Jeff would be secure. The attack was vicious as described to me by Jeff, but minimized in the press. The chaplain, I learned after Jeff's death, had also reassured Jeff's minister, Roy Ratcliff. Whether the chaplain was acting in an official contact capacity or not we do not know, but Mr. Ratcliff and I agreed that we were lulled into a secure feeling and we felt betrayed upon hearing of Jeff's murder. I also felt guilty. I might, I thought, have probed the warden or others regarding security after that first unsuccessful attempt on Jeff's life.

I found out recently that, amazingly, Jeff was allowed to be without supervision for some twenty to forty minutes with a man who had previously attacked other people at another Wisconsin prison using makeshift weapons. This man also repeatedly threatened to kill white people. One report in July 1994 described this person together with a threat on Jeff specifically, but CCI personnel concluded that it was not substantive.

After surprising Jeff from behind and bludgeoning him to death with a 20 by 2½ inch metal bar, this person crossed the gym area, in full view of the security cameras, and made good on his past repeated threats by murdering Jesse Anderson, as well. The murder investigation is supposedly complete and only one person has been charged. As of this writing, the prison system has given no information regarding the following:

1. An inmate wrote to Jeff's attorney, Steve Eisenberg, saying there was complicity and there was a "hit squad."
2. Jeff and Jesse were dropped off for work detail at 8:00 am November 28, 1994, and the person charged with their murders, at 8:05 am. Then, no one

can account for anybody from 8:05 to 8:40 am, including the whereabouts of the guards and the recreation director. What about sounds and screams, which are sure to have occurred?

3. Cameras are everywhere, always rolling, and monitored in a central control room. What happened?

4. Why would a person with a history of making racial threats and attacking people with makeshift weapons in prison even be allowed in the vicinity of a metal bar? Or the broom he was carrying? Or be allowed to be anywhere near people he specifically threatened?

We will have to wait to see what comes out of the panel formed by the director of Wisconsin's prisons, after they "review CCI policies and procedures."

Even though Jeff is dead, everything continues to play in my mind. Problems still have to be dealt with, such as the dogged court efforts by a Milwaukee attorney to auction off the instruments of crime. Fortunately, several family members of Jeff's victims realize the ramifications and have stood firm with us to voice opposition. A European friend told me that not only would such an auction not be allowed in his country, but it would be considered to be crossing over the line of acceptable behavior.

Two other lawsuits against me have been in progress for over a year, much like the one described earlier with Shari. I have become very disillusioned and hurt by the process.

And so, as these cases and other things drag on, costing emotions and money, I wonder why they weren't summarily dismissed. It seems strange to me that the probation department case was dismissed when their required but nonexistent visitations might have caused Jeff to be discovered much sooner.

Other things seem unfair or regrettable. I still remember how Jeff agonized to me about "giving in" when a Milwaukee psychologist appeared early one morning at CCI and pressed Jeff to sign over his rights to the many hours of interviews. The psychologist had told him, Jeff said, that the material would be used only for teaching purposes (classes). When the material showed up in a commercial book, Jeff felt betrayed and manipulated, as I did when the detailed family history, which I supplied in confidence to help Jeff in the insanity defense, showed up in the same book.

I guess I felt as if I betrayed Jeff, as well, when he asked me one day, "Dad, how come your book didn't have more of the happy things we did together?" He was referring to the two years of 4H we shared raising lambs, building fences for them, planting gardens, hiking in metropolitan parks, sharing science fair plans, etc. My weak reply was that the book was intended to show a limited focus, a spiraling down-ward. Jeff said, "It sure did that all right."

I felt that I unknowingly betrayed Jeff when I urged that an insanity plea would be his best bet at getting effective psychological treatment. Everyone connected with Jeff's defense concurred. After the trial, however, I learned from reliable sources that mental treatment at the state psychiatric institutions was essentially custodial and the physical conditions abysmal, perhaps a combination for totally sending Jeff off the deep end. I thought, Shouldn't this have been known? I asked rhetorically, "What was the Milwaukee trial really for?"

If I had known then what I learned after the trial I would have urged for no trial on the basis of insan-ity. Brian Masters gives an excellent assessment of the true nature of the trial, the jury, and all the machina-tions which took place.

But now, in light of what happened at CCI, a place designed to prevent just exactly what occurred, it seems to me that there was no appropriate place for Jeff to go, except where he is now, with his Lord.

—Lionel H. Dahmer
March 1, 1995

CPSIA information can be obtained
at www.ICGtesting.com
Printed in the USA
LVHW101503031022
729844LV00006B/264